DIVIDEND INV___ ___
&
SWING TRADING

A Complete Guide on Investing, Options, Day Trading,
Forex Trading, Future Trading, Dividend Growth Investing
and Passive Income for Early Retirement

JOEY THOMPSON

Table of Contents

DIVIDEND GROWTH INVESTING

A Step-by-Step Guide to Building a Dividend Portfolio for Early Retirement

By Joey Thompson

INTRODUCTION

Any individual looking to invest some cash in stable returns must have heard of dividend investing and the opportunities that it offers. We all want to follow the footsteps of the likes of Bill Gates and Warren Buffet and earn a stable monthly passive income. Perhaps not as much, but only a fraction of what their ROIs look like would be great to have!

But here's the truth - those passive incomes did not come from passive decisions. There is a reason why most investors are avid readers - they learn before they apply. And you need to do the same. In order to yield stable returns, you need to know the ins and outs of investing in dividends.

No matter what professional stage you are at, it is always important to have an idea about various investment options before you put your money on the line. Many investors don't begin their research regarding investments until they are about to reach retirement. Retirement, however, is the ideal time to REAP the benefits of those investments, not the ideal time to make them. Does it mean that you can't generate a stable income post-retirement? Of course not! It just means the sooner you begin, the higher your returns will be in the long run.

Dividend investing is more than just a pastime and is often considered a stream of passive income with little to no effort required. Sure, that will come too, but before you can get to that point, you need to know the inside outs of dividend investments. You need to know exactly what companies to invest in and when. You need to be able to read tables and understand the influence of the economic and political conditions of a country that influence the market rates. Not to say you need to ditch your work and spend all your time reading books and watching newspapers. But just one rightly put together report, like this book, can help you make smarter and profitable investment decisions with dividends.

The purpose of developing an ebook for dividend investment growth was to serve as a guide for new and existing investors that have a particular interest in receiving regular income. I will begin with a brief explanation of the term dividend, expanding onto its types, important terms and procedures involved in it, and eventually, provide guidance to build an effective dividend portfolio.

CHAPTER 1

HOW DIVIDEND INVESTMENT WORKS?

What is a Dividend?

A dividend is a return on shares that a company pays its shareholders from its corporate earnings. Any and every successful business requires consistent cash flow to thrive. When investors buy shares of a company, they receive dividends or returns on the investment. Investors, also known as shareholders, invest in the hope of generating consistent returns in the future.

History of Dividend Investment

The emergence of dividend policy dates back to the 13th century when a French bank Société des Moulins du Bazacle offered dividends to its shareholders. Continuing to the 17th century, Dutch East India Company (VOC) became the first public entity to offer a regular dividend payout. For nearly two decades, VOC

4

continued paying approximately 13% of its share values to the shareholders. Although the dividend payout options were still low up until the 18th century, more companies introduced the polices pertaining to the industrialization and business growth.

Types of Dividends

Most companies have a Board of Directors as well as external and internal share and stakeholders. These Share and stakeholders are one way or the other directly influenced by the economic performance of the company. These stake and shareholders hold a little chunk of the company, in the form of shares. And thus, they also receive a share of the profits; one method of receiving those profits is known as dividends.

Dividend distribution can happen in one of many forms. The following are the five different ways dividends are distributed among the shareholders.

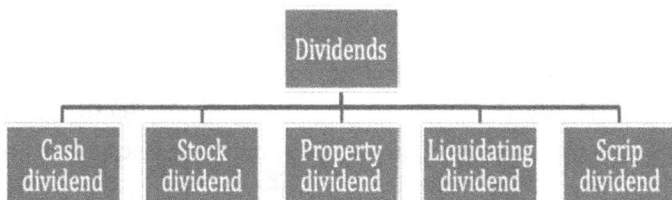

```
              ┌────────────┐
              │  Dividends │
              └────────────┘
   ┌──────┬──────┬──────┬──────┬──────┐
┌──────┐┌──────┐┌──────┐┌──────┐┌──────┐
│ Cash ││Stock ││Prop. ││Liqui.││Scrip │
│divid.││divid.││divid.││divid.││divid.│
└──────┘└──────┘└──────┘└──────┘└──────┘
```

Cash Dividend

A cash dividend is when the company decides to pay back a small percentage of its earnings to its stakeholders in the form of cash. By making a cash dividend, the company's share price takes a dip. The price drop is often equal to the amount of the dividend.

Example

For instance, a company offers a cash dividend equal to 6% of its stock price. When the investor or stakeholder cashes out this profit, the stock price too drops by 6%. This drop is caused by the economic value transfer.

Stock Dividend

This is a suitable strategy for investors looking to invest long term. With this strategy, the company reinvests the dividends earned back into buying more stocks for the shareholders. Usually companies opt for this when they are short of cash flow or would like to hold on to the profits for further investment.

Property Dividend

Property dividends are paid in the form of assets, unlike the other two options that pay off in the form of cash or stock. Property dividend distributions are recorded at the fair market value of the 'property' or assets that are distributed. Fair market values are not the same as the book value of the asset and because of this slight difference, the company has the liberty to record that little variance as either a loss or gain, so as to alter their reported and taxable incomes.

Example

The company XYZ decides to issue special 500 identical signed prints by Pablo Picasso, which the company has kept stored in its vault for some years. The prints were acquired by the company for $500,000 and as of the date of dividend declaration, they happen to have a fair market value of $4,000,000. XYZ records the following entry as of the declaration date to record the change in the value of assets along with the liability to pay the dividends.

	Debit	Credit
Long-term investments-artwork	3,500,000	
Gain on appreciation of artwork		3,500,000
Retained Earnings	4,000,000	
Dividends Payable		4,000,000

On the date of dividend payment, XYZ records the following entry to record the payment transaction

	Debit	Credit
Dividends Payable	4,000,000	
Long-term investments-artwork		4,000,000

Scrip Dividend

It is possible that a company may not have the sufficient resources or funds to issue dividends in the near future. Therefore, it issues a scrip dividend, which is basically a promissory note (may or may not include interest) to pay shareholders at a later date. This dividend creates a note payable.

Example

XYZ international declares a scrip dividend of $250,000 to its shareholders at 10% interest rate. At the date of the dividend declaration, it records the following entry:

	Debit	Credit
Retained Earnings	250,000	
Notes Payable		250,000

Since the date of payment is one year later, XYZ has accrued an interest expense of $25,000 on notes payable. On the date of payment (assuming there is no previous or prior accrual of interest expense), the following entry is recorded by XYZ:

	Debit	Credit
Notes Payable	250,000	
Interest Expense	25,000	
Cash		275,000

Liquidating Dividend

This happens when the company decides to return the invested capital back to their shareholders. This often happens when the company is about to shut down and thus wants to return the investments. Calculations and process for liquidating dividends are similar to those of cash dividends, with the only difference that the funds are considered to come from the additional paid-in capital account.

When are Dividend Stocks Distributed?

Dividend dates are important to keep track of because they are a source of regular income. In understanding the process and distribution of dividends, it is important for the investor to know about the important dates including the declaration date, record date, ex-dividend date and the payment date.

The following section mentions and explains various important terms related to dividend earning. In order to understand the process, you need to understand these important terminologies.

Declaration Date

Every company selects a date for the dividend payout which is known as the declaration date. Details such as the record and payment date, size of dividend and other relevant details are provided in the declaration statement and are released along with the payment. Declaration date is also known as announcement date.

Example

Company XYZ declared dividend of $0.258 per size of dividend on June 15, 2019, and therefore it is recorded as the declaration date. This is different from the payment and record date which will be explained in the next section. The decision of the declaration date is taken by the board of directors and is disseminated to all the relevant shareholders.

Record Date

Also known as the cut-off or book closure date, the record date is the specific day when the company decides to pay the dividends to its shareholders. People often confuse it with the ex-dividend date and the easiest way to remember the difference is by understanding that ex-dividend date is set by the stock exchange and record date is set by the company and the former occurs prior to the record date.

The shareholders for a company are not constant. New shareholders keep adding up as well as opting out and therefore it is important to ascertain the list of shareholders on a specific date. This also helps to eliminate the shareholders that have opted out so that the funds are appropriately distributed.

The record date is also important because it has a special relationship with the ex-dividend date. It is thereby important to understand that the record date may slightly differ between various stock exchanges such as the New York Stock Exchange and London Stock Exchange. In order for you to be in the record books, it is important to buy the stock at least 2 working days prior to their record date. This is because when the investor purchases stock from the exchange, it takes a while to update the details of the investor on the company's books. Normally the settlement period is based on the formula of T+2 which means that it takes two business days for the stock trading to settle.

For John to receive the dividend from the company XYZ on the record date, it is important that he should buy the stocks at least two business days before the record date or the ex-dividend date that occurs a day before the date of record.

The Ex- Dividend Date

One of the most important dates to consider is the ex-dividend date. It refers to exactly a day before the dividend record date and the first day when trade of stocks takes place without dividend. This date is set by the stock exchange where the trading takes place and the company has no role in setting the ex-dividend date.

Its calculation is based on the $T + 2$ system of settlement prevalent in North America which takes 2 business days to settle the stock trades after the transaction is completed. In case the investor buys the stock one working day before the record date, the stock trade settlement will take place in one working day after the record date. Therefore, the investor will not receive the dividend for that particular month. There are, however, exceptions to this rule. For example, if the value of dividend is more than 25% or above then the payment may take longer to process, but that hardly ever happens.

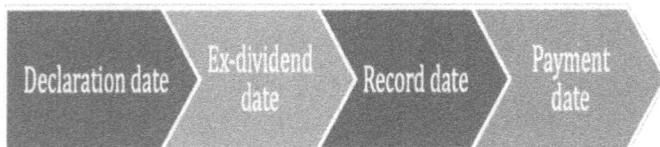

Declaration date > Ex-dividend date > Record date > Payment date

Dividend Yield

Not every company has a payout dividend policy. Therefore, the annual payout is the percentage of return which the company pays in relation to the share price. The dividend yield is taken as a positive key indicator of a company's growth because only the successful companies share their earnings. A simple formula to calculate the dividend yield is by dividing the annual dividend per share with the current price of the stock. The resulting amount is presented as a percentage.

Dividend yield= (Annual dividend/Stock price) * 100

Example

The company XYZ page out an annual dividend of $ 5.89 and its current stock price is $ 25.00. Applying the relevant formula, the company's dividend yield would be:

Dividend yield= (Annual $1.44/$53 * 100= 2.7 percent

It must be noted that the stock dividend yield is not constant due to the fluctuations in the market. Also, it is paid only when the company decides to do so.

Payment Date

As the name implies, the payment date is the date when the shareholders receive the dividend. There are various ways in which shareholders receive the dividend payments, including electronic transfer to the shareholder's account or a cheque being directly mailed to the investor. Companies around the world have different payment schedules. The US companies pay four times a year, whereas other international companies pay once or twice a year.

Dividend Reinvestment Plan (DRIP)

This term refers to the reinvestment of dividends into additional shares and is done automatically. This is useful in situations where the shareholders receive a small number of dividends. For the investor considering selling the stock with DRIP, it is important to consider the ex-dividend dates because the inability to do so will generate residual shares that the seller may not be looking forward to.

For instance, John purchases 50 shares of the company XYZ at a price of $23. This yields a dividend of $0.47 per share on a quarterly basis. If the stocks do not have a DRIP policy, the amount will be insufficient to buy stocks in the case of the DRIP plan; the dividend amount will then be reinvested to buy further stocks.

DRIP has a few advantages, such as the entire income generated from the dividend can be reinvested, and there is no commission to be paid. The stockholder must get the complete information of DRIP from the broker so that they are able to receive the advantage without any delay.

Accelerated Dividend

The amount of dividend paid before any changes in the dividend policy is known as an accelerated dividend. For instance, if there is a change in the tax rate of dividends, the company will release the payment earlier so that the changes do not affect the shareholders in a negative manner.

Example

For instance, the UK Treasury introduced a new tax policy on dividends on April 6, 2016. The policy entailed that the first payout of £ 5000 as dividend income will not be taxed. However, if this amount exceeded, the shareholder was liable to pay 7.5% of tax. Similarly, the taxpayer was supposed to pay 32.5% and 38.1% to be paid by the additional rate taxpayer. The marginal rate tax for the shareholders was increased to approximately 6% under this policy. In case that the company considered paying the accelerated dividend before April 6, the shareholders would be saved from paying a fraction of the liable taxes.

Special Dividend

Also known as the extra dividend, the special dividend is the amount that a company pays to its shareholders apart from the regular income distributed as per the dividend policy. This payment is non-reoccurring and is paid only once. The amount paid under a special dividend policy is greater than the regular dividend income. The shareholder receives this in case the company yields higher profits than it initially expected, or there have been other specific circumstances, like a special payoff, resulting in higher yield for the investors.

When a company has an excess of cash available on its balance sheet, and it does not plan to reinvest that cash in the business, the company may distribute the amount among its shareholders as a special dividend. For instance, Microsoft paid a special dividend of $3 per share in 2004. It was a onetime offering with the total value of the payout of $32 billion.

The company may also use a special dividend to further strengthen the bond of trust and loyalty with its customers. These complimentary offerings help gain the trust and loyalty of the shareholders. The ultimate purpose of investing in the stock is for you to have a source of regular income. Therefore, additional cash is always welcome by the shareholder. Think of it as a bonus but with the exception that there is no additional work involved.

If the company plans to alter its financial structure, it can release a special dividend by reducing the assets and equity of the company. As the special dividend is paid out, the company successfully alters the percentage of equity and percentage of the debt.

The cyclical companies often adopt the hybrid dividend policy in which a special dividend is paid along with the regular dividend since the companies are significantly affected by the changing economic situation.

The special dividend is paid only if the company has earned better profits and it is safer to adopt this policy rather than changing the dividend rate because in case of economic slowdown or recession, the company may have to decrease the dividend percentage and it often does not settle well with the shareholders.

Trade Date

It is a date when you purchase the stock by paying the complete amount. Trade dates play an important role in how taxes are collected. Taxes are usually calculated based on trade dates.

Settlement Date

It is the date that is decided between the buyer and seller for sale and purchase. Most commonly, it takes three working days for the stocks to settle after the trade has been carried out, and the seller and buyer have to share the stocks and make a payment, respectively, within those three working days.

Why Do Companies Increase Dividend?

When companies have a surplus amount of profit, they can distribute or invest those profits in multiple ways, dividends being one of those options. The decision, however, comes from the board of directors, and options are explored, keeping in view various factors. The following section lists various options for the company to consider.

If the value of company stocks is good, the company may repurchase them back from the investors. This reduces the percentage of shares floating in public, but doing so can be risky if the company fails to make anticipated profits in the long run.

Companies may look into paying off their debt by using profit through stock trade. This can help in the reduction of interest payments for the company.

Companies may also look into sharing profits with investors in terms of dividends. This decision, however, depends upon the type of management. If it desires to share its profits, it can do so in terms of dividends payout. The company can reinvest its earnings to develop further and enhance the company's growth.

This increase in dividends benefits both the company and the shareholders. The company is able to retain its shareholders while the investor is able to make stable and consistent growth in their profits. At the end of the investment, the initial amount of investment remains the same, while returns gradually increase.

There are two ways for an investor to make money with stock investments. The first method is where the stock prices take an immediate hike. Say an investor purchases 100 stocks at the price of $35 for each stock; say the price increases to $60 per stock in just 24 months. This means that there has been an unrealized capital gain. If the investor sells the stocks at the end of those two years, he is likely to realize again.

The other way is to get returns through dividends, and therefore the investor is likely to become an owner of a small portion of the company's corporate earnings. Dividends are decided by the board of directors and are most commonly paid quarterly.

An Example

Consider the well-known company Microsoft that did not adopt a dividend payment policy until its business gained momentum. The process took several decades to develop, and currently, it offers one of the highest paying dividends among other technological companies. The stocks have also witnessed unprecedented growth over the period of time, and investors have established trust in the company's performance.

Dividends are corporate earnings of a company which it distributes to the shareholders. The companies, however, are under no obligation to do the same. Companies like Google and Facebook do not have a dividend payout policy, whereas relatively younger companies prefer to reinvest their earnings. The companies that are more established tend to have dividend policies.

Factors that Influence Dividend Payout for Companies

There are well-established companies that do not prefer to share their corporate earnings with the shareholders because they find much more value in reinvesting for the growth of the business. Also, there may be a preference for avoiding the high cost associated with issuing new stocks and rather reinvest the earnings.

Increased Profits

When a company has a surplus profit, it may look into investing in further growth opportunities, making acquisitions, buying back its own shares, or debt payment. On the other hand, companies having less, or medium-scale earnings may not offer shares. There is a possibility that the companies making huge earnings want to share their profits with the investors.

For instance, the retired workforce has a particular interest in dividend policies since it offers a steady and lucrative stream of passive income. However, even for the investors, there are drawbacks of receiving dividends, the fact that they are taxable being one of the more significant ones.

Established companies that pay out dividends depict a prosperous and performance-oriented futuristic approach. It sends out a strong signal to the public that it is financially strong and willing to share its earnings with the people. A gesture of goodwill is created as well as the investors maintaining a trust level and loyalty towards such companies. Dow Jones, Verizon, Wells Fargo, and Eon Mobil are some of the companies that have successfully rolled out their dividend policies and have a strong investor build up.

Financial Discipline for the Company

Dividend policy may prevent a company from misallocating its capital. It also drives managers to work harder for the company. The investors expect higher yields in the form of dividend payouts. A dividend manager is in charge of creating sustainable and profitable cash flow for the investors and the company.

Paying out dividends helps keep the company's finances in control. A company may end up reinvesting the profits in less lucrative opportunities and thus fail to create healthy cash flow. Timely payment of dividends allows the company to offer consistent returns on the investments shareholders have made with them while creating financial discipline within.

Separation of Power

Another reason to have a dividend policy is to create a barrier between ownership and management. Dividends are proof that a company is into sustainable income growth. The board of directors is usually responsible for determining the payout ratio that needs to be shared with investors.

Aversion of Market Risks

It is a known fact that the value of dividends tends to grow with time. Companies that have been running successfully for many years have higher-yielding payouts compared to newer companies. Such companies have been in the business for more than 25 years and are often known as the dividend aristocrats. With shares in possession of investors, the company may also be able to buy them back in case of an economic recession. However, it is important to understand that investing in dividends does not guarantee consistent returns. There may be times when markets will fluctuate, and so will the payouts.

Financially strong companies pay dividends on a regular basis and keep on increasing the number of cash payouts in order to keep up with inflation. This is similar to receiving a hike in salary or increasing rent from your tenants in case you have a property rented out. It is, therefore, better to go with such stable companies so that the investors do not feel the pinch of inflation and continue to receive better returns.

Ability to Attract Investors

Dividends are essential in attracting investors. Companies offer dividends so as to lure investors in to invest in their business. Investors looking for ways to invest their money in a passive, yet stable stream will find dividend investments an ideal opportunity, most commonly to secure their retirement plans.

Companies require hefty amounts to set up, operate, and smoothly run a large business. Having that cash flow enables them to collect cash and then payout when the company is able to yield returns on those investments.

Searching for an Effective Dividend Policy

While choosing the stocks, many investors look at the current yield instead of the total return value. This may result in overlooking the balance sheet of the company, along with the potential consistency of learning the payout ratio. Therefore, it is important that in order to select the right company to invest in, its history must be thoroughly checked to ensure that the company has been paying a dividend on a regular basis. This reduces the risk of investing in a company that has a history of reduction in dividend returns or even elimination. The investor must consider a few characteristics while selecting the company to invest in by looking at its deliverables, especially during the economic slowdown. The following section lists the qualities that an investor must look at while building the dividend portfolio.

Having a keen eye on the changing economic landscape and business opportunities is a good way to start. A lot of online sources provide a diverse range of information that can be overwhelming and confusing, to say the least. This section covers everything you need to know before screening companies for dividend investments. Please note that these are general guidelines and cannot truly determine the credibility or the effectiveness of a company to offer desirable returns. However, thorough research will help you make informed decisions in this regard.

Greater Annual Growth Rate

The annual growth of the dividend must be greater than the current rate of inflation. Ideally, the dividend growth ratio must be prioritized against the average dividend offering. Knowing that the annual growth rate is higher than the inflation rate ensures that your investments will remain profitable and will increase in value over time.

There are exceptions to this rule. Say the annual inflation rate is at 4%, and the company is offering a stable 12% return. But the returns will remain consistent for the next three years. At first glance, it would seem as if the growth rate is not increasing each year, but in reality, the results would be better than a dividend return of 4% the same year with an annual growth of 2%. In this case, though, the investor would yield the same amount of returns for the next three years, but the overall profits would be much higher than a company offering increasing growth rates at a lower rate.

Needless to say, there aren't a one shoe fits all model of investment; whether you plan on becoming an active or passive investor, you will actively need to study each candidate company thoroughly.

Continuous Dividend Growth

The dividend portfolio must include companies that have at least 5% of dividend growth over a period of 10 years because that shows that the company is financially strong and will be able to give comparatively better payouts even during an economic slowdown. The best way to analyze that is to consider the performance of the company during the reception and expansion period. Avoid investing in new companies even if they show a strong alliance with well-established companies because such investments can be riskier.

Low Volatility

The stocks have a volatility rate in comparison to the market. This is known as the Beta rate, and it describes the risk ratio of the relevant stocks. It is important to consider that the stocks have a rather stable position in the market. Those stocks that significantly fluctuate possess a higher risk. The market consists of 1.0 beta and provides a scale of ranking for the stocks in the market. Those about 1.0 are riskier but can yield higher returns. The low beta stocks possess low yields as well as having a lower risk factor.

Learning how to measure beta is important for an investor. The basic formula for calculating beta is Beta=Variance/Covariance, and this is done by incorporating aggression analysis.

It is of utmost importance to analyze the volatility level of the stocks so that the risks are analyzed before making a purchasing decision. Of course, trust your knowledge and experience as well in establishing a clear decision but keep the beta ratio in mind as well.

All these terminologies may seem overwhelming initially. But once you get the hang of it, you'll be talking and walking the investor lingo in no time! Another word of caution: beta analysis of a particular stock does not depict the future returns and therefore, must not be considered as a final analysis because of other factors that influence the market, such as the index, inflation, and economic stability.

A few examples of the companies with a low beta ratio include AT&T with 0.56 and Colgate Palmolive with a

0.43 beta rate. These are well established and economically sound companies that have been in the market for decades and have gone through fluctuations and survived. As a new investor, it may be difficult to assess the volatility ratios correctly. As a rule, just make sure that the volatility ratio of stocks must be less than 1.0 in order for you to even consider investing with them.

Risk Assessment

An interesting tip to consider from the father of value investing, Benjamin Graham, is that while looking for stable stocks to invest in, one must look out for the margin of safety, a term that is used to differentiate the companies that have stood against economic fluctuations or instabilities. In doing so, the investor must look at the balance sheet of the company as well as the dividend growth ratio over a period of time. Make sure that there is no instance of overpaying because that can mean a high-risk level associated with stocks.

Don't Put All the Eggs in One Basket

It may become overwhelming while one is on a look-out for effective dividend payout policies. People tend to rush and invest as much as they can in a certain company's stocks, but that may not be the most suitable solution. At any given period of time, certain economic conditions and activities may slow down the growth of a specific company or even an entire industry or sector, whereas; the same economic conditions may become favorable for other industries.

In a situation like this, an investor with a diversified portfolio is able to sail through those fluctuating conditions without being affected. So unless you haven't promised your loyalties and your money to a specific company or industry (don't you ever!), you'd be better off having a diversified portfolio.

A quick look at investment portfolios of the top 10 or 10,000 investors even would help you understand the importance of diversification. Also, make sure that you don't just invest in different companies operating in the same sector, diversify in terms of industries too. For instance, if the price of crude oil increases by 20% overnight, then the entire transportation industry would be negatively affected, not just a specific airline. Hence, selecting multiple industries (more on that later) would help you create a stable and economically proof portfolio.

CHAPTER 2

CHOOSING YOUR HIGH PERFORMING DIVIDEND STOCKS

Dividend Aristocrats

The dividend aristocrats consist of the 50 companies that have shown a significant increase in their dividend payout for the past 25 years. There is a certain criterion that the stocks must fulfill in order to become part of this list and must also be listed at the S&P 500. If an investor is looking for performance, consistency, and predictability, then this index is the go-to-place. Mostly, the dividend aristocrats are the blue-chip companies and have been committed to a steady and consistent dividend payout growth over many decades.

The criteria that a company must meet in order to become part of the list include the following:

- The company must show a dividend payout growth of at least 25 consecutive years.

- The company's stocks must be listed on the S&P 500.

- The company must have a certain market cap and fulfill certain liquidity requirements.

The aristocrat companies are good investment options because the stocks under this umbrella are mostly defensive and can sail through their difficult economic situations. One of the main reasons these companies are a viable option is because they have been able to build credibility and thus would always have a steady stream of income coming in from trusting investors, helping them stay afloat. Another important factor is that their dividends have been increasing for the past 25 years, giving them a competitive advantage over other companies.

As an investor, you must understand that these companies are not recession-proof. However, their performance and cash flow have not been significantly affected by an economic slowdown. For example, during the 2008 recession, the aristocrat companies had a decline of 22%, whereas the S&P 500 accounted for a loss of 38%. Hence, as an investor, it is a safer bet to invest in these companies since they have outperformed over the past few decades and adjusted their returns after facing the market risks.

Falling Out of the Aristocrat Index

This index is maintained by Standard and Poor (S&P) company, and it keeps adjusting the criteria every year in January. The companies that make up the index have to maintain their position and are added and taken off the index as per their situation.

How to Invest in the Aristocrat Index

There are many websites that provide the list of aristocrat companies and provides the required information to the investors to help them with their decision making. These websites have a number of criteria for the investors to select from. These websites offer valuable information regarding a company's position on the aristocrat index and how often it has fluctuated. You want to look for a company that has been able to retain its position over different economic conditions for it to be a viable option.

These companies are always under pressure with respect to their performance, and they often buy back their stocks in case of an outperformance. However, for the investors looking for a consistent income stream as well as dividend growth, the aristocrat index is worth referring to.

A common perception is that dividend-paying stocks always outperform the non-dividend-paying stocks because:

- This gives out the message that the company is shareholder-friendly since it rewards them in the form of cash payments.

- These companies take a lot of consideration while spending on the growth projects because they are issuing some of their earnings to the shareholders, and therefore such companies cannot afford to make any risky decisions. In other words, the capital allocation of the search company is already highly scrutinized.

- The companies that pay a dividend to the shareholder are likely going to focus on business growth so they can generate cash earnings in order to reward the shareholders, and therefore the riskiest stocks are already excluded.

The most recent analysis shows that sector-wise the consumer staples and industrials topped the aristocrat index. Next in line is the information technology sector that has significantly paved its way up to the list.

Company	Dividend Yield	Annual Payout	Payout Ratio	3-Year Dividend Growth	P/E Ratio
3M	3.56%	$5.76	60.06%	7.01%	20.74
A. O. Smith	2.21%	$0.96	38.71%	0.00%	19.44
Abbott Laboratories	1.62%	$1.44	39.89%	10.75%	43.06
AbbVie	5.79%	$4.72	49.95%	22.62%	37.59
AFLAC	2.04%	$1.08	24.27%	7.47%	13.05
Air Products & Chemicals	1.93%	$4.64	49.15%	6.88%	28.22
Archer Daniels Midland	3.07%	$1.40	N/A	0.00%	21.62
AT&T	5.57%	$2.08	57.78%	2.00%	16.73
Automatic Data Processing	2.09%	$3.64	59.00%	0.00%	32.00
Becton Dickinson and	1.13%	$3.16	25.12%	2.43%	71.96
Brown-Forman	1.02%	$0.70	N/A	0.00%	38.67
Cardinal Health	3.62%	$1.92	38.17%	1.58%	-3.77
Caterpillar	3.05%	$4.12	38.61%	9.95%	12.82
Chevron	4.29%	$4.76	68.10%	3.29%	15.93
Chubb	1.96%	$3.00	27.15%	2.08%	19.45

Cincinnati Financial	2.11%	$2.24	55.58%	0.00%	19.17
Cintas	0.91%	$2.55	33.55%	0.00%	33.09
Clorox	2.72%	$4.24	68.94%	8.93%	24.69
Colgate-Palmolive	2.48%	$1.72	57.53%	2.65%	25.71
Consolidated Edison	3.14%	$2.96	65.49%	3.50%	22.27
Dover	1.65%	$1.96	31.11%	2.50%	26.74
Ecolab	0.95%	$1.88	28.88%	0.00%	38.09
Emerson Electric	2.72%	$2.00	54.95%	1.28%	19.79
Exxon Mobil	5.40%	$3.48	100.58%	4.38%	18.73
Federal Realty Investment Trust	3.36%	$4.20	120.69%	0.00%	37.04
Franklin Resources	4.17%	$1.08	42.19%	9.17%	11.01
General Dynamics	2.25%	$4.08	31.70%	0.00%	15.69
Genuine Parts	3.17%	$3.05	51.69%	4.15%	17.67
Hormel Foods	1.94%	$0.93	53.14%	11.00%	26.61
Illinois Tool Works	2.43%	$4.28	53.77%	14.38%	23.21
Johnson & Johnson	2.54%	$3.80	41.71%	4.60%	22.10

Kimberly Clark	2.86%	$4.12	56.91%	2.02%	23.12
Leggett & Platt	3.26%	$1.60	62.50%	0.00%	22.12
Linde	N/A	N/A	0.00%	0.00%	N/A
Lowe's Companies	1.85%	$2.20	32.93%	13.12%	31.40
MCCORMICK & CO /SH	1.50%	$2.48	46.36%	0.00%	31.54
McDonald's	2.32%	$5.00	58.96%	9.29%	28.32
Medtronic	1.84%	$2.16	38.57%	0.00%	34.01
Nucor	3.34%	$1.61	40.97%	2.10%	11.64
Pentair	1.73%	$0.76	29.69%	N/A	20.78
People's United Financial	4.54%	$0.71	51.82%	1.08%	12.33
PepsiCo	2.67%	$3.82	64.09%	6.44%	16.37
PPG Industries	1.67%	$2.04	30.18%	6.27%	23.46
Procter & Gamble	2.38%	$2.98	59.60%	2.90%	74.20
Roper Technologies	0.53%	$2.05	15.11%	13.56%	35.32
S&P Global	0.77%	$2.28	21.86%	11.61%	35.40
Sherwin-Williams	0.80%	$4.52	18.59%	9.96%	38.00

Stanley Black & Decker	1.69%	$2.76	30.63%	4.48%	35.47
SYSCO	2.18%	$1.80	47.12%	10.89%	25.31
T. Rowe Price Group	2.24%	$3.04	35.14%	10.06%	17.23
Target	2.31%	$2.64	38.37%	2.66%	18.23
The Coca-Cola	2.73%	$1.60	71.11%	2.63%	32.58
United Technologies	1.93%	$2.94	33.79%	2.63%	23.88
VF	2.28%	$1.92	53.93%	0.00%	26.25
W W Grainger	1.83%	$5.76	32.95%	0.00%	18.43
Walgreens Boots Alliance	3.53%	$1.83	31.23%	5.69%	12.72
Walmart	1.82%	$2.12	42.48%	1.29%	23.23[1]

Historical data of dividend yield growth per company [2]

Company Name	No. of Years	Dividend Yield	Current Price	Annual Dividend
American States Water	65	1.36%	$89.97	$1.2200
Dover Corp.	64	1.70%	$116.45	$1.9600

[1] https://www.marketbeat.com/dividends/aristocrats/
[2] https://www.dividend.com/dividend-stocks/10-year-dividend-increasing-stocks/

Northwest Natural Gas	64	2.51%	$75.58	$1.9100
Genuine Parts	63	3.17%	$96.58	$3.0500
Emerson Electric	63	2.71%	$74.43	$2.0000
Procter & Gamble	63	2.39%	$126.03	$2.9836
3M	61	3.24%	$165.58	$5.7600
Cincinnati Financial	59	2.14%	$105.35	$2.2400
Johnson & Johnson	57	2.55%	$149.50	$3.8000
Lowe's	57	1.84%	$121.15	$2.2000
Lancaster Colony Corp.	57	1.72%	$159.93	$2.8000
Coca-Cola Co.	57	2.78%	$57.01	$1.6000
Illinois Tool Works	56	2.47%	$175.86	$4.2800
Colgate-Palmolive	56	2.45%	$69.71	$1.7200
Chubb Limited	54	1.99%	$150.96	$3.0000
Hormel Foods	53	1.99%	$47.05	$0.9300
Tootsie Roll	53	1.05%	$34.12	$0.3600
ABM Industries	52	1.90%	$39.12	$0.7400
Federal Realty Investment Trust REIT	52	3.30%	$127.23	$4.2000
Stepan Co.	52	1.07%	$102.07	$1.1000
Target	52	2.29%	$115.44	$2.6400

Stanley Black & Decker, Inc.	52	1.64%	$166.35	$2.7600
California Water Services Group	52	1.49%	$53.19	$0.7900
SJW Corp	52	1.61%	$74.16	$1.2000
Commerce Bank shares	51	1.54%	$68.30	$1.0400
Black Hills Corp	50	2.59%	$82.85	$2.1400
H.B. Fuller Co.	50	1.33%	$48.56	$0.6400
National Fuel Gas Co.	49	3.93%	$42.79	$1.7400
Sysco Corp	49	2.15%	$82.67	$1.8000
Becton Dickinson	48	1.13%	$282.26	$3.1600
Leggett & Platt	48	3.22%	$50.21	$1.6000
Mine Safety Applications	48	1.23%	$138.64	$1.6800
Tennant Co.	48	1.06%	$80.72	$0.8800
Universal Corp	48	5.65%	$53.41	$3.0400
W.W.Grainger	48	1.79%	$323.45	$5.7600
Abbott Labs	47	1.61%	$89.54	$1.4400
Gorman-Rupp	47	1.54%	$37.73	$0.5800
PepsiCo	47	2.66%	$142.44	$3.8200
PPG Industries	47	1.62%	$124.03	$2.0400
V.F. Corporation	47	2.25%	$83.63	$1.9200
AbbVie Inc.	47	5.62%	$83.77	$4.7200

Middlesex Water Co.	47	1.54%	$66.30	$1.0250
Helmerich Payne	47	7.03%	$40.64	$2.8400
Kimberly-Clark	47	2.97%	$144.89	$4.2800
Nucor Corporation	46	3.11%	$49.47	$1.6100
Automatic Data Processing	45	2.07%	$178.30	$3.6400
Telephone & Data Systems	45	2.62%	$24.30	$0.6600
Consolidated Edison	45	3.28%	$94.18	$3.0600
Wal-Mart Stores	45	1.83%	$116.60	$2.1200
RPM International	45	1.94%	$72.98	$1.4400
MGE Energy	44	1.76%	$80.46	$1.4100
Walgreens Boots Alliance, Inc.	44	3.43%	$52.78	$1.8300
Pentair Inc.	43	1.62%	$44.28	$0.7600
Archer Daniels Midland Co.	43	3.27%	$42.66	$1.4000
McDonald's	43	2.34%	$210.39	$5.0000
Carlisle Co.	43	1.29%	$156.39	$2.0000
RLI Corp	43	1.00%	$94.87	$0.9200
Clorox Co.	42	2.65%	$156.07	$4.2400
Medtronic, Inc.	42	1.79%	$119.18	$2.1600

Sherwin Williams	41	0.76%	$591.05	$4.5200
Eaton Vance	39	3.28%	$46.62	$1.5000
Community Trust Bancorp	39	3.38%	$44.64	$1.5200
Sonoco Products	39	2.90%	$58.38	$1.7200
Franklin Resources	38	4.38%	$25.09	$1.0800
Old Republic International Corp	38	3.53%	$23.08	$0.8000
Weyco Group	38	3.98%	$23.93	$0.9600
Air Products & Chemicals	37	2.30%	$236.45	$5.3600
Exxon Mobil	37	5.21%	$64.74	$3.4800
Aflac	37	2.08%	$52.37	$1.0800
Atmos Energy	37	1.98%	$116.31	$2.3000
Cintas Corporation	37	0.92%	$277.96	$2.5500
Brown-Forman	35	0.99%	$70.47	$0.6972
Donaldson Company	35	1.59%	$53.18	$0.8400
AT&T	35	5.38%	$38.58	$2.0800
Ecolab Inc.	34	0.96%	$198.18	$1.8800
First Source Corporation	34	2.34%	$48.79	$1.1600
Brady Corp	34	1.54%	$56.89	$0.8700

Mercury General	34	5.24%	$48.83	$2.5200
Chevron Corp	34	4.31%	$111.12	$4.7600
UGI Corp	34	2.95%	$43.00	$1.3000
Universal Health Realty Income Trust REIT	34	2.19%	$125.95	$2.7400
Tompkins Financial	34	2.28%	$87.95	$2.0800
McCormick & Co.	33	1.44%	$166.06	$2.4800
T. Rowe Price	33	2.28%	$131.30	$3.0400
First Financial Corp	33	2.38%	$42.80	$1.0400
Cullen Frost Bankers Inc.	27	3.09%	$92.88	$2.8400
Tanger Factory Outlet REIT	27	8.66%	$14.95	$1.4200
West Pharma Services	27	0.41%	$157.33	$0.6400
John Wiley & Sons	26	2.94%	$45.97	$1.3600
Essex Property Trust REIT	26	2.52%	$308.41	$7.8000
Expeditors International	25	1.35%	$73.85	$1.0000
Erie Indemnity	24	2.31%	$167.75	$3.8600
Artesian Resources Corp. - Ordinary	24	2.63%	$38.00	$0.9984

Shares - Class B				
New Jersey Resources Corp.	24	2.87%	$43.15	$1.2500
Realty Income Corp REIT	24	3.61%	$78.13	$2.7900
TJX Companies	23	1.47%	$61.30	$0.9200
General Dynamics Corporation	22	2.23%	$183.63	$4.0800
Southside Bancshares	22	3.37%	$36.09	$1.2400
Computer Services, Inc.	21	1.65%	$51.30	$0.8400
First Robinson Financial Corp.	21	1.97%	$62.01	$1.2000
CCFNB Bancorp Inc.	21	3.20%	$49.15	$1.5600
Roper Industries	21	0.54%	$377.90	$2.0500
Enterprise Products Partners L.P.MLP	21	6.61%	$27.24	$1.7800
Urstadt Biddle Properties REIT	20	4.60%	$23.42	$1.1200
Muncy Bank Financial Inc	20	3.41%	$42.00	$1.4000
IBM Corp	20	4.67%	$139.55	$6.4800

Owens & Minor	20	0.15%	$6.65	$0.0100
Brown & Brown, Inc.	19	0.82%	$44.65	$0.3400
Nu Skin Enterprises	19	3.92%	$34.55	$1.4800
W.P. Carey Inc. REIT	19	4.93%	$83.77	$4.1520
Badger Meter	18	1.12%	$61.45	$0.6800
National Bank shares	18	3.47%	$41.38	$1.4400
McGrath Rent Corp	18	1.94%	$79.00	$1.5000
Republic Bancorp	18	2.62%	$44.48	$1.1440
The J.M. Smucker Company	18	3.25%	$106.27	$3.5200
Vanguard Total Stock Market ETFETF	18	2.10%	$166.17	$3.5420
York Water	18	1.45%	$48.78	$0.7208
Banc First Corp	18	2.15%	$59.53	$1.2800
Bunge Ltd.	18	3.86%	$51.61	$2.0000
Donegal Group Inc. Cl B	18	4.06%	$12.40	$0.5100
Microchip Technology	18	1.33%	$104.20	$1.4660

Farmers & Merchants Bancorp	18	1.86%	$770.54	$14.3000
Southern Company	18	3.60%	$70.05	$2.4800
Atrion Corp	17	0.86%	$717.93	$6.2000
Avista Corp.	17	3.12%	$49.99	$1.5500
Oil-Dri Corp of Americia	17	2.74%	$35.80	$1.0000
Lockheed Martin	17	2.22%	$437.17	$9.6000
Lindsay Corporation	17	1.21%	$101.95	$1.2400
Casey's General Stores	17	0.77%	$163.49	$1.2800
Harris Corp	17	0.00%	$189.13	$0.0000
ONEOK Inc.MLP	17	4.90%	$75.05	$3.7400
Occidental Petroleum	17	7.43%	$41.20	$3.1600
Calvin b. Taylor Bankshares, Inc.	17	3.47%	$35.75	$1.2400
Perrigo Company	17	1.41%	$59.52	$0.8400
Ritchie Bros. Auctioneers	17	1.85%	$43.20	$0.8000
Costco	16	0.84%	$310.85	$2.6000
Chesapeake Utilities	16	1.69%	$95.86	$1.6200

Holly Energy Partners L.P.MLP	16	11.25%	$23.69	$2.6900
Microsoft	16	1.22%	$165.46	$2.0400
Texas Instruments	16	2.68%	$128.04	$3.6000
VSE Corp	16	1.05%	$32.90	$0.3600
Waste Management	16	1.69%	$121.05	$2.0500
Assurant, Inc.	16	1.97%	$129.49	$2.5200
Albemarle Corp	16	1.86%	$80.20	$1.4700
Bank Of Utica - Ordinary Shares (Non Vtg.)	16	3.56%	$435.00	$15.5000
Eagle Financial Services, Inc.	16	3.30%	$31.50	$1.0400
Delhi Bank Corp	16	2.18%	$33.25	$0.7296
J.B. Hunt	16	0.94%	$112.86	$1.0800
Jack Henry & Associates	16	1.07%	$150.05	$1.6000
Lincoln Electric	16	2.15%	$93.13	$1.9600
Silgan Holdings	16	1.39%	$31.42	$0.4400
Prosperity Bancshares	16	2.66%	$67.72	$1.8400
Xcel Energy	16	2.42%	$67.22	$1.6200

Westlake Chemical Co.	16	1.55%	$64.20	$1.0500
Rollins Corp	16	1.15%	$36.73	$0.4200
Robert Half International	16	1.98%	$61.05	$1.2400
Torrington Water Co.	16	3.12%	$41.00	$1.2800
Edison International	15	3.35%	$76.80	$2.5500
BOK Financial	15	2.55%	$80.31	$2.0400
iShares S&P 1500 Index Fund (ETF)ETF	15	2.02%	$73.77	$1.4725
Bank Of Utica	15	2.73%	$567.27	$15.5000
Hawkins, Inc	15	2.20%	$42.35	$0.9200
Kellogg Co.	15	3.30%	$68.98	$2.2800
Landstar Systems	15	0.66%	$112.08	$0.7400
Lyons Bancorp, Inc.	15	3.26%	$38.77	$1.2400
Royal Gold Inc.	15	0.99%	$111.72	$1.1200
UMB Financial	15	1.87%	$65.35	$1.2400
Verizon	15	4.07%	$60.70	$2.4600
Alerus Financial Corp	15	2.49%	$21.49	$0.5600
AmerisourceBergen Corp	15	1.83%	$89.11	$1.6000

Cass Information Systems	15	1.90%	$56.84	$1.0800
J&J Snack Foods	15	1.25%	$165.01	$2.3000
Graco Inc.	15	1.36%	$55.05	$0.7000
General Mills	15	3.68%	$53.01	$1.9600
Cardinal Health	15	3.61%	$53.80	$1.9244
Digital Realty Trust REIT	15	3.35%	$129.82	$4.3200
Renaissance Re Holdings	15	0.71%	$189.94	$1.3600
Church & Dwight	14	1.26%	$72.02	$0.9100
American Financial Group	14	1.66%	$109.20	$1.8000
Flowers Foods	14	3.48%	$21.58	$0.7600
iShares Core S&P U.S. Growth ETFETF	14	1.49%	$69.95	$1.0260
Portland General Electric	14	2.57%	$60.91	$1.5400
Raytheon Co.	14	1.64%	$227.62	$3.7700
A.O. Smith	14	2.19%	$45.49	$0.9600
Jardine Strategic Holdings Ltd.	14	0.00%	$32.27	$0.0000

Northeast Indiana Bancorp Inc.	14	2.63%	$41.00	$1.0800
Alliant Energy	14	2.58%	$59.15	$1.5200
CenterPoint Energy	14	4.39%	$26.31	$1.1500
Technology Select Sector SPDRETF	14	1.20%	$96.93	$1.1787
First of Long Island Corp	13	3.09%	$23.13	$0.7200
First Community Financial Corp	13	4.88%	$22.11	$1.0800
C.H. Robinson Worldwide	13	2.60%	$77.88	$2.0400
Duke Energy	13	3.93%	$96.21	$3.7800
Axis Capital Holdings	13	2.65%	$62.26	$1.6400
OGE Energy	13	3.38%	$45.79	$1.5500
Tomra Systems ASA	13	0.00%	$28.80	$0.0000
Aaron's Inc.	13	0.26%	$62.77	$0.1600
Kerry Group Plc - Ordinary Shares - Class A	13	0.76%	$129.85	$0.9840
People's United Financial	13	4.42%	$15.85	$0.7100
Ross Stores	13	0.86%	$114.48	$1.0200

Broadridge Financial Solutions	12	1.67%	$129.77	$2.1600
Warrior Met Coal Inc.	12	1.02%	$19.56	$0.2000
Healthcare Services Group	12	3.05%	$26.25	$0.8000
Hillenbrand Inc.	12	2.85%	$30.23	$0.8500
Northrop Grumman	12	1.38%	$381.84	$5.2800
Aqua America Inc.	12	1.80%	$52.15	$0.9372
Experian Plc	12	1.84%	$35.36	$0.6500
The Ensign Group	12	0.45%	$45.78	$0.2000
Philip Morris International	12	5.37%	$84.68	$4.6800
Thomson Reuters	12	1.83%	$80.38	$1.4400
Evercore Partners	11	3.18%	$73.49	$2.3200
Chemed Corp	11	0.27%	$477.97	$1.2800
Coca-Cola European Partners Plc.ADR	11	2.61%	$52.99	$1.3800
Artesian Resources	11	2.56%	$39.25	$0.9984
American Water Works Company	11	1.48%	$135.80	$2.0000

Invesco Ltd.	11	7.01%	$17.97	$1.2400
Prudential Financial	11	4.19%	$92.00	$4.0000
North Western Corp.	11	3.05%	$75.87	$2.3000
Quaint Oak Bancorp Inc	11	2.40%	$15.00	$0.3600
Power Shares QQQETF	11	0.82%	$221.45	$1.8306
Travelers Co.	11	2.44%	$134.39	$3.2800
Western Gas Partners L.P.MLP	11	12.99%	$18.18	$2.4880
Arrow Financial	11	2.90%	$35.82	$1.0400
Bank of Marin Bancorp	11	2.02%	$45.50	$0.9200
Monro Muffler	11	1.18%	$70.85	$0.8800
Horace Mann Educators	11	2.67%	$43.52	$1.1500
New Market Corp	11	1.64%	$448.21	$7.6000
Altria Group	11	6.65%	$50.17	$3.3600
Isabella Bank Corp	11	4.46%	$24.25	$1.0800
Dominion Resources	11	4.51%	$84.52	$3.7600
Kroger	11	2.26%	$28.33	$0.6400
Unum Group	11	3.98%	$27.34	$1.1400
Visa	11	0.58%	$202.85	$1.2000

Ryder System	11	4.23%	$49.80	$2.2400
Techtronic Industries Co. Ltd. - ADR	11	1.26%	$41.33	$0.5340
iShares Dow Jones Select Dividend Index Fund ETF	10	3.40%	$105.63	$3.5660
Eaton Corp	10	3.00%	$96.27	$2.8400
BlackRock, Inc.	10	2.52%	$529.97	$13.2000
Caterpillar Inc.	10	3.04%	$136.74	$4.1200
Cummins Inc.	10	3.18%	$166.08	$5.2440
CSX Corp	10	1.28%	$76.22	$0.9600
Cognex	10	0.40%	$54.91	$0.2200
Chico's FAS	10	9.23%	$3.99	$0.3500
Armanino Foods Of Distinction Inc.	10	2.95%	$3.25	$0.1000
TD Ameritrade	10	2.60%	$48.35	$1.2400
FedEx	10	1.75%	$148.40	$2.6000
Analog Devices	10	1.92%	$114.31	$2.1600
Applied Industrial Technologies	10	1.99%	$65.56	$1.2800
Bar Harbor Bank shares	10	3.82%	$22.91	$0.8800

Hershey Company	10	2.02%	$152.19	$3.0920
HEICO Corp	10	0.13%	$123.16	$0.1600
Hasbro Inc.	10	2.62%	$104.99	$2.7200
iShares Russell Top 200 Growth Index Fund ETF	10	1.03%	$100.17	$1.0196
iShares Dow Jones U.S. Total Market Index Fund ETF	10	1.84%	$162.30	$2.9612
Oxford Industries	10	2.03%	$70.97	$1.4800
Pfizer	10	3.73%	$38.14	$1.5200
Quaker Chemical	10	0.92%	$169.00	$1.5400
Norfolk Southern	10	1.80%	$204.76	$3.7600
National Retail Properties REIT	10	3.64%	$56.49	$2.0600
Omnicom Group	10	3.30%	$76.76	$2.6000
Maxim Integrated Products	10	3.02%	$62.09	$1.9200
MDU Resources Group	10	2.76%	$29.67	$0.8300
Lakeland Bancorp	10	2.98%	$16.73	$0.5000

Marsh & McLennan Corporation	10	1.59%	$115.14	$1.8200
Republic Services	10	1.72%	$94.36	$1.6200
Retail Opportunity Investments Corp REIT	10	4.48%	$17.13	$0.7880
Rockwell Automation	10	2.02%	$196.67	$4.0800
Risk George Industries, Inc. - Ordinary Shares - Class A	10	3.81%	$10.50	$0.4000
Simon Property Group REIT	10	5.70%	$139.99	$8.4000
SPDR Series Trust - SPDR Portfolio Large Cap ETF	10	1.93%	$38.44	$0.7516
Standex International Corp	10	1.12%	$76.91	$0.8800
UDG Healthcare Plc	10	0.82%	$10.85	$0.0892
Union Pacific	10	2.07%	$179.64	$3.8800
UDR Inc. REIT	10	2.84%	$48.20	$1.3700
Domtar Corp	10	4.60%	$36.76	$1.8200

UnitedHealth Group	10	1.44%	$285.87	$4.3200
Tri-Continental Corp.	10	11.19%	$28.67	$3.2460
Taubman Centers REIT	10	8.55%	$28.50	$2.7000
SPDR S&P 500ETF	10	1.89%	$326.89	$6.2800
Charles Schwab U.S. Broad Market ETFETF	10	2.33%	$78.06	$1.8492
Susquehanna Community Financial Inc	10	8.27%	$19.80	$1.6400
Spirent Communicatio ns Plc - ADR	10	1.09%	$12.19	$0.1379
Six Flags Entertainment	10	8.91%	$37.73	$3.3200
Vanguard Information Tech ETFETF	10	1.00%	$258.88	$2.6052
Waste Connections	10	0.76%	$98.25	$0.7400
WR Berkley Corporation	10	0.62%	$72.37	$0.4400
Williams Sonoma	10	2.54%	$74.72	$1.9200
Ameriprise Financial	10	2.39%	$165.12	$3.8800
Compagnie financiere	10	1.53%	$7.57	$0.1152

Richemont SA - ADR				
Brookfield Infrastructure Partners L.P.MLP	10	3.71%	$54.49	$2.0100
Autoliv Inc.	10	3.34%	$78.24	$2.4800
Broadcom Limited	10	4.21%	$318.31	$13.0000
Coca-Cola European Partners Plc	10	0.00%	$46.72	$0.0000
Cracker Barrel	10	3.33%	$156.86	$5.2000
Bristol-Myers Squibb	10	2.83%	$64.81	$1.8000
Henderson Land Development Co. Ltd. - ADR	10	2.24%	$4.65	$0.1024
Hawthorn Bancshares	10	2.00%	$23.58	$0.4800
National Health Investors REIT	10	4.89%	$85.38	$4.2000
Moody's Corp	10	0.78%	$260.19	$2.0000
NextEra Energy, Inc.	10	1.92%	$265.81	$5.0000
Littelfuse Inc.	10	1.04%	$186.77	$1.9200
Legg Mason	10	4.16%	$39.50	$1.6000
Magellan Midstream	10	6.35%	$63.91	$4.1100

Partners L.P.MLP				
Industria De Diseno Textil SA	10	2.58%	$34.10	$0.8800
Kentucky Bancshares, Inc.	10	2.92%	$23.25	$0.6800
Franklin Electric	10	1.05%	$59.95	$0.6200
Idex Corp	10	1.18%	$171.28	$2.0000
International Flavors & Fragrances	10	2.24%	$135.45	$3.0000
Iron Mountain REIT	10	7.82%	$31.96	$2.4740
Group 1 Automotive	10	1.12%	$104.49	$1.1600
Pioneer Bank shares Inc	10	3.05%	$28.86	$0.8800
Omega HealthCare Investors Inc. REIT	10	6.20%	$43.40	$2.6800
KLA Tencor	10	2.00%	$175.93	$3.4000
Northrim Ban Corp	10	3.50%	$37.97	$1.3200
United Parcel Service	10	3.28%	$115.37	$3.8400
Scotts Miracle-Gro Co.	10	2.14%	$109.30	$2.3200
Steris Corp	10	0.97%	$151.05	$1.4800

Snap-On	10	2.56%	$164.80	$4.3200
Paccar Inc.	10	1.65%	$76.77	$1.2800
Health Care Select Sector SPDRETF	10	1.62%	$102.18	$1.6876
Vanguard Mid-Cap ETFETF	10	2.16%	$181.08	$3.9648
Regal-Beloit Corp	10	1.42%	$81.70	$1.2000
SEI Investments	10	1.07%	$63.45	$0.7000
Thor Industries	10	1.92%	$82.08	$1.6000
Tiffany & Co.	10	1.73%	$134.09	$2.3200

REITS

Real Estate Investment Trusts (REITs)

The REITs operate differently from other securities. Companies under the REITs umbrella are obliged to pay out 90 percent of their earnings to the shareholders in the form of dividends. Various REIT options are available in the market and the investor is required to carry out extensive research because not all companies yield higher payouts.

REITs require the shareholders to pay tax and therefore the companies are exempt from doing so. These are considered to be relatively safe investments and are often significantly influenced by market conditions and recession but otherwise the yields are lucrative. Historically, REITs have provided reliable returns on income, enabled wealth accumulation, protection from inflation as well as reduced portfolio volatility.

Top REIT Dividend Stocks [3]

Brookfield Property REIT Inc Class AREIT	6.97%	$19.14	$1.3200	2019-11-27	2019-12-31
Kite Realty Group	6.96%	$18.36	$1.2700	2019-12-19	2019-12-27
Taubman Centers, Inc. Preferred Shares Series J	6.30%	$25.68	$1.6250	2019-12-13	2019-12-31
Ramco-Gershenson Properties Trust Preferred Shares	6.12%	$58.91	$3.6250	2019-12-19	2020-01-02
SITE Centers Corp.	5.89%	$13.23	$0.8000	2019-12-12	2020-01-07
Simon Property Group	5.70%	$139.99	$8.4000	2019-11-14	2019-11-29
Kimco Realty Corp	5.56%	$20.20	$1.1200	2019-12-31	2020-01-15
Brixmor Property Group Inc	5.50%	$20.79	$1.1400	2020-01-03	2020-01-15

[3] https://www.dividend.com/dividend-stocks/financial/reit-retail/#tm=3-industry-stocks&r=ES%3A%3ADividendStock%3A%3AStock%23RPT-PR-D--NYSE&f_2=reit-retail

Weingarten Realty	5.10%	$30.48	$1.5800	2019-12-05	2019-12-13
Monmouth Real Estate Investment Corp	4.60%	$14.84	$0.6800	2020-02-14	2020-03-16
Getty Realty Corp	4.58%	$32.18	$1.4800	2019-12-24	2020-01-09
Retail Opportunity Investments Corp	4.48%	$17.13	$0.7880	2019-12-13	2019-12-30
Urban Edge Properties	4.44%	$19.41	$0.8800	2019-12-13	2019-12-31

New investors are often suggested to begin their investment portfolio with the accumulation of stocks. The safe and stable dividend income generation happens through utility organizations or the telecommunication sector. These companies are known for their high dividend yield as well as the ability to encounter economic instability. Companies such as Verizon and AT&T have a higher payout ratio of over 6% whereas Duke Energy pays 5% or above to its investors.

In order to build a stellar dividend portfolio, you need to find the top companies offering high dividend yield for its stocks. Consider companies that have high corporate earnings and share a significant amount of the earnings with the shareholders as dividends. You should invest some time and effort in understanding how various sectors perform and which industries offer the most stable returns on the investments. You need to be on the lookout of industries that withstand fluctuation economic conditions.

Websites like www.dripinvesting.com are the ultimate source to receive the names and information of the industries as per your criteria. Another way to consider the relevant companies is to look for the industries that have always been in demand for their products and services.

Utility sector is often considered the most lucrative since no matter what the economic conditions, people will continue to purchase basic utilities. Other popular sectors include telecom and real estate; again these are basic needs and need to be addressed and catered to no matter how the economy is doing. For instance, even during economic slowdown people will still buy soaps and use communication services and therefore these industries have a higher chance of sailing through tough economic conditions.

The companies that have less predictable earnings are likely to pay because the capital might be needed in a downturn. It is also difficult for those companies to plan their cash flow in advance and the economic volatility makes the environment much more skeptical. Similarly, companies with higher predictable earnings give out more to their shareholders.

Telecommunications

Telecommunications equities are the most preferred investments and can resist economic instabilities while maintaining a stable income flow. Telecommunications is an amalgamation of various complex structures including telephones, Internet and mobile phones. The heavy dependence of people on these systems makes the sector highly valuable and no matter what happens around the world, these services are essential in staying in touch and caring about day-to-day business activities.

In the past, telecommunications consisted of national operators but with the emergence of mobile technology, companies are earning their revenues through data packages and mobile plans. These companies pay out higher dividends and have more accumulated cash and are projected to yield higher earnings in the foreseeable future. Because of the growing demand for telecommunications and services, this sector has become highly monopolized by the governments but operates as an independent business entity because of the significant infrastructure involved.

The telecommunications sector consists of medium and large-scale companies such as AT&T and Verizon. These companies are big enough to withstand the exorbitant amount of expenditure involved in the expansion, operation and maintenance costs involved. Despite the challenges, the telecommunication sector has been able to adapt technological innovations and advancements and therefore continues to yield a steady dividend payout. However, the investment must be careful enough not to consider the newly established or small-scale companies because they are often unable to maintain the maintenance cost and therefore the dividend payout and growth potential is less.

Considering that AT&T and Verizon are the key players in telecommunications sector, below is a graphical representation of dividend growth for these companies from 2009 to 2017[4].

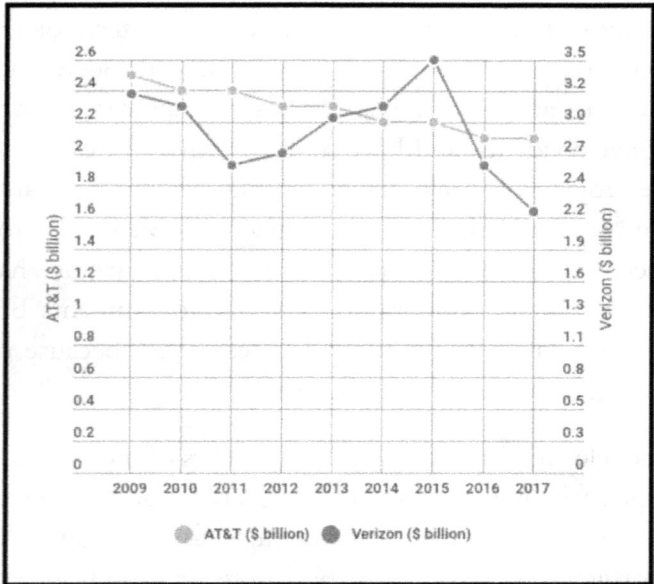

[4] https://www.dividend.com/how-to-invest/7-charts-that-compare-att-and-verizon-t-vz/

Consumer Staples

Food, beverages and items for daily use make up the consumer staples category. These are essentials that consumers cannot part ways from regardless of their financial status. Even during economic recession, these items remain in demand and therefore give out a continuous income stream. This is one of the most favored categories for investors especially during unstable economic conditions. Well-known companies including Coca Cola, Procter & Gamble and Nestle are some of the companies that fall under this category.

Tobacco

The tobacco industry is safe, and it has survived quite a many economic upheavals in the past. Although the earnings are not even, the investors are fortunate to profit from dividend growth as well as increased stock prices. Let's consider an example to analyze this sector. British American Tobacco is reported to pay out $2.68 per share on an annual basis. The dividend yield is reported at 6.11% while the company is known to pay out 67 percent of its corporate earnings as dividends, BTI has managed to increase dividends every year[5].

---

[5] https://www.marketbeat.com/stocks/NYSE/BTI/dividend/

Quarterly dividend history of British American Tobacco (NYSE:BTI)- 2013-2020

Announced	Period	Amount	Yield	Ex-Dividend Date	Record Date	Payable Date
3/1/2019	quarterly	$0.6745	7.11%	12/26/2019	12/27/2019	2/11/2020
3/1/2019	quarterly	$0.6745	7.11%	10/3/2019	10/4/2019	11/19/2019
3/1/2019	quarterly	$0.6745	7.11%	6/27/2019	6/28/2019	8/13/2019
3/1/2019	quarterly	$0.6745	7.11%	3/21/2019	3/22/2019	5/13/2019
2/23/2018	quarterly	$0.6792	4.33%	12/27/2018	12/28/2018	2/12/2019
2/23/2018	quarterly	$0.6792	4.33%	10/4/2018	10/5/2018	11/20/2018
2/23/2018	quarterly	$0.6792	4.33%	6/28/2018	6/29/2018	8/13/2018
2/22/2018	None	$0.6740	4.33%	3/22/2018	3/23/2018	5/14/2018
12/5/2017	None	$0.5810	1.73%	12/28/2017	12/29/2017	2/13/2018
7/27/2017	None	$0.7280	2.28%	8/16/2017	8/18/2017	10/3/2017
7/27/2017	None	$0.7280		8/16/2017	8/18/2017	10/3/2017
3/2/2017	semiannual	$1.4771	4.63%	3/15/2017	3/17/2017	5/9/2017
8/1/2014	semiannual	$1.6041	2.76%	8/20/2014	8/22/2014	10/3/2014
3/3/2014	semiannual	$3.2645	6.02%	3/12/2014	3/14/2014	5/13/2014
8/2/2013	semiannual	$1.3641	2.51%	8/21/2013	8/23/2013	10/3/2013

Utilities

Utilities, like consumer staples, are another stable sector to include in a dividend portfolio. The utility sector includes companies that have a defensive business cycle that will operate no matter how difficult the market becomes. In other words, these companies will never have to close their operations even in the case of an economic slowdown. These include electricity, gas and water supplies among other basic daily utilities.

The revenue will continue to flow and since they operate on a cost-plus model, these companies are able to maximize their rate of return. For instance, water, electricity and gas will never lose their value to the people and are essential utilities in everyday use. Since this industry requires a significant amount of infrastructure, the debt is also on the higher side. The performance of their finances are positive if the interest rates are low.

Although various factors have overshadowed utilities in terms of highest paying dividends, it still remains as one of the important means of income generation for investors. The utility sector is most suitable for conservative investors, but the companies that have a higher ratio of dividend payout mean that the dividend growth potential is limited. Overall, this sector tops the list of suitable sectors to include in one's portfolio due to its unchanging and ever-increasing demand.

Master Limited Partnerships (MLPs)

MLPs encompass the limited partnership that is publicly traded. The companies that come under this sector deal in crude oil, natural gas and storage tanks. The MLPs have a higher yield compared to the utilities sector because these operate on the toll road system, in which the revenues generated are based on fee structure. MLPs consist of both energy and non-energy related companies and include gas and oil industries and also includes the industries that produce fertilizers and timber.

These companies enjoy a lot of tax exemptions; for instance, a company can qualify as an MLP if 90% of its income is generated from activities based on natural resources. Also, the revenue generated is based on the volume of gas oil that passes through the pipelines and not dependent upon the price of the fuel and therefore fluctuation in the market price of fuel does not have an adverse impact on the sector. Because of these advantages, MLPs are able to distribute high dividend payout among shareholders in most scenarios.

To Conclude

All these industries have their pros and cons. While many can withstand economic conditions, the investor is still at the mercy of a company's performance to yield desirable returns. If, for whatever reason, the company isn't able to sustain profits, the investor is left hanging dry with nothing to own as a token of its loyalty. Say a share of a dividend drops from $62 to $8 or less, there is nothing that an investor is left with. Hence, the risk factor remains high and can raise alarm at any given point.

The only way an investor can withstand these risks or ensure that he doesn't lose everything that he has invested in, he needs to invest in something more concrete, like real estate. And that is where REITs become interesting. They allow investors to skip the hassle of becoming property investors and all the troubles and processes this entails and yet be able to enjoy lucrative and sustainable profits of a real estate investor.

CHAPTER 3

STRATEGIES AND PROS AND CONS

Pros and Cons of Dividend Investing

On the one hand, where dividends are meant to benefit the shareholders, they tend to carry some disadvantages as well. You will need to know both sides of this coin inside out before you can make informed decisions. In this section, we go through all the advantages and disadvantages of investing in dividends that you, as an investor, need to understand before putting your money on the line.

Generate Passive Income

The biggest upside to dividend investing is that you can create a steady stream of income and even create immense wealth with little to no effort on your part. Sure, you will have to do your homework and be aware of market conditions to understand how your investments are doing, but in the long run, you'll just sit back, relax and enjoy the fruits of your investments, minus the labor.

Although expecting the dividend-paying companies to do good with their dividend payouts continuously may seem risky, the fact is that well-established companies and organizations tend to go to extreme lengths to keep their dividends both predictable and healthy. They go to great lengths to ensure that dividend payouts equal or exceed inflation levels year after year. Hence, they do the hard work while you enjoy the **benefits.**

Take Full Advantage of Compounding

Compounding is a pretty useful way to increase your income by investing what you earn in order to generate more earnings. It is a process in which one does not have to make additional investments to gain more earnings. Instead, allow the earnings to do the entire work for you. In the case of dividends payout, when you opt to purchase additional dividends, you are, in fact, increasing your earnings because every dividend has its own regular payout, which will continue to compound over time.

So all you really need to do is invest an initial amount and then let the profits from those investments create more profits and start the snowball rolling.

Invest Once and Profit Twice

By investing in dividend stocks, you tend to gain benefits in more than one way. We are already well aware of the regular payouts one receives while investing in dividend stocks, but they also happen to be a return on investment when the share prices increase. non-dividend-paying stocks will only benefit you once when and if you purchase them at a lower price and then sell them at a higher price. Dividend stocks, on the other hand, will provide you a share of the company's profit and allow you to retain the ownership of your investment as well. And since the well-established companies tend to be financially strong and reliable, their stock prices tend to increase over time, **increasing the confidence of their shareholders as well.**

Return Maximization with Dividend Reinvestment

We already know that you can achieve higher returns and earnings if you are using the compounding technique. However, it can be easier and more convenient if you happen to use a dividend reinvestment plan.

The dividend reinvestment plan happens to be a program that allows the investor to automatically invest their cash dividends back into purchasing additional company shares, DRIPs this way combine the benefits of both compounding and dollar-cost averaging.

These automatic purchases of shares usually occur at the payment date of the company's dividends and can be managed by the stock company itself or by a broker or an outside agent.

Full Enrollment

There may be a full enrollment in DRIP. For instance, John owns 1,000 shares of Coca Cola, and the dividend paid annually on each share is $ 1.56. The current value of the stock trade is $47 per share. The company has already paid a quarterly dividend of 39 cents.

Before John enrolled himself in the DRIP, his account would receive $ 390 on a quarterly basis. However, this time he owns $ 1,008.29 in shares. This means that the dividend of $ 390 has been fully enrolled or reinvested, whereas the fractional shares of Coca-Cola stand at $47 per share.

Partial Enrollment

John owns 500 thousand shares of a company in which the annual dividend rounds up to $3.20 per share and the trading value per share is $49. Out of the total dividend payout which John receives on a quarterly basis, he would like to reinvest and considered partial enrollment of 300,000 shares. In this case, when John receives the quarterly dividend payout, $ 160,000 will be paid in the form of cash. An additional 4,898 will also be received by John as per the following calculations:

300,000 * $0.80 = $240,000 / $49 = 4,898

Stock Market Insulation

One of the many advantages offered by investing in dividends is insulation from the stock market, which means that your investment will not, in any way, be influenced by stock market conditions. Since predicting the stock market is almost impossible and not easy, investing in dividends is a more feasible investment option for investors with good expected returns.

Dividends Mean That You Will Not Have to Sell Shares to Gain a Return

The stock market happens to be fair when it comes to valuing businesses. In other words, if the share of the company you have invested in is increasing, so will the value of your investment. But what happens when the stocks, for whatever unforeseeable reasons, take a major dip? What happens to your investment? It goes from sky-high to ground low with nothing to show for your years of investment. Say you were investing for retirement. And the dip happens right before retirement, and you are left with no money and no time to generate a stable income.

On the other hand, dividends offer regular payouts, so even in a case where the market does plunge, you will have generated a good return on your investment by then.

Dividends Support the Stock Price

It has been found that dividends support stock prices during times of recession. Dividend-paying stocks also outperform during bear markets and recessions. The reason behind dividend stocks outperforming when the market is performing poorly is because if the share prices fall, the investors will be drawn to buy more into the stocks due to the yield alone. In addition to that, since interest rates are also significantly influenced when the markets are performing poorly, dividend stocks offer risk-free rates, making them more of a viable option.

Dividends Prevent Misallocation of Capital

When investors are investing in dividend stocks of the company, they not only expect to be paid in return but also expect that the dividends will grow. Therefore, managers in such cases do all they can in order to make sure that the company is able to pay back the dividends to its shareholders and further increase their confidence.

Dividends Taxed at a Lower Rate

Dividends happen to be more tax efficient as compared to bonds and other investment options. People who lie in lower brackets do not pay federal income tax on dividends. And for individuals who are below the 35% mark on the income tax bracket, the dividends are only taxed at 15%. Even though it cannot be said that the same tax favoring situation will last forever, it definitely is a bonus for dividend investors.

Some Pitfalls and Risks Associated with Dividend Growth Investing

Twice Taxation

One of the main drawbacks of dividend investing is that the dividends are subject to being taxed twice. The first instance is when you receive the dividends because the company that is paying them is paying dividends from its net income on which it has to pay tax on annual earnings. The second instance of taxation occurs when you, as an investor, must pay personal income tax on any dividends you earn during the tax year. This means that you are paying tax twice, once being a partial owner and the other as an individual.

Growth Rate

This is an important consideration when screening companies for investments. The growth rate highlights the rate at which a specific company's stock price is affected over a period of time. Investors need to assess the history of dividend rate's growth when making purchasing decisions. Since reducing dividend rates can negatively impact the company's stock price, a company will likely increase dividends only in cases where it can sustain the higher payouts.

The growth rate is calculated by checking the percentage of the dividend that a company has increased annually.

Dividends are Not Guaranteed Unlike Interest

It is often said that dividends are the "new interest," though this is not totally correct. Interest happens to be contractually agreed, whereas dividends happen to be voluntary payments made by the corresponding companies, which can be deleted at any time. Since dividends are basically a company sharing its profit with the shareholder, a company will only pay them if it has gained any profit.

Effects of Dividend Policy Changes

When a company that is paying dividends makes certain changes to its dividend policies, especially when it comes to cutting or eliminating payouts, it is going to have a negative effect on the stock price of the company. It is a well-known fact that investors are hugely concerned with the dividend policies and any changes that may take place. Therefore, they will be drawn to sell or purchase dividends based on what changes are made to the dividend policies. If a company intends to cut its dividend payouts, the investors will receive lower earnings.

Investors Cannot Control Dividends

Unlike stocks, investors of dividends have absolutely no control over the payout methods of their investments. For instance, if the company decides to switch their payout from cash to property or liquidation, then there is very little that the investor can do to control their investment returns.

Strategies for Successful Investing

Dividend Growth Investing

Any investor is not looking at short term gains but also the long term returns for his investment. If you are investing in REITs, then you will also monitor the price of your investment. The value of stocks, as well as the value of your property, should gradually and consistently increase.

When investing in dividends, opt for companies that have a higher potential for growth. Your portfolio should include companies that are well-established and can offer consistent results, but also some companies that have major growth potential. These are relatively riskier than investing in seasoned companies, but can also offer higher returns in the long run.

A good rule of thumb would be to keep a certain percentage for investing in companies with higher growth potential. For instance, you could decide to keep 30% of your investments for such companies, and this way, if the company or number of new companies do well in the stock market, you yield higher returns. However, if they fail to grow at the desired or expected rate, then it won't break your bank.

Dividend Capture Strategy

This strategy is income-focused, where investors deal with stock trading. This is an ideal strategy for day traders. Unlike more common strategies of buying and holding consistently paying dividend stocks to yield stable income, this is a strategy that requires active trading. An investor purchases and sells shares more frequently in the hope of receiving dividends on every stock before selling them again. In some cases, this can mean holding on to a stock for just a day even.

Investors for this strategy opt for dividends that payout annually in order to generate larger payouts. This is a suitable strategy for someone who is willing to either actively get involved or would like to partner with a seasoned trader to make quick decisions regarding their investments. A trader will need to read and calculate dividend payouts on dividend calendars in order to assess the right time to buy and sell dividends profitably on a short-term basis.

CHAPTER 4

SHOULD YOU BUY REITS?

According to the reports of S&P Global Market, REIT stocks have been one of the most benefitting investments within the past decade. At the moment, the dividend yield of REITs has been 4 percent, whereas the rate per share has gone up to 32 percent. It is not wrong to say that since the Great Depression, REITs have done quite well as property investments have always been on the rise all around the world.

One such example is of Simon Property Group Inc. that has increased per share dividend cash payout by $2. Similarly, Alexandria Real Estate Equities and Omega Healthcare Investors Inc. have also reportedly increased their dividend payout significantly.

Outperformance- Reasons

In recent times, there has been a drastic decrease in bond investments as the returns remain quite low. Most investors have relocated their assets to higher dividend-paying entities and have benefited from it. Most of this relocation has been REITs due to their stable and higher returns.

Moreover, since REITs are supposed to distribute 90 percent of their income to their shareholders, the dividend payout, as well as the yields, are higher in proportion. The chart below reveals the current status of the highest yielding REITs that have continuously increased and maintained a higher dividend payout trend.

Company	Ticker	Dividend yield	FFO Yield	'Headroom'	Total return - 12 months
Macerich Co.	MAC, +2.38%	10.26%	12.36%	2.60%	-37%
Iron Mountain Inc.	IRM, +0.76%	7.19%	6.27%	-0.92%	15%
Simon Property Group Inc.	SPG, -0.26%	5.31%	7.97%	2.66%	-6%
Kimco Realty Corp.	KIM, +0.68%	5.24%	6.69%	1.45%	53%
Host Hotels & Resorts Inc.	HST, +0.06%	4.77%	10.73%	6.02%	-7%
Weyerhaeuser Co.	WY, -2.52%	4.67%	1.70%	-2.97%	11%
Ventas Inc.	VTR, +0.10%	4.40%	5.43%	1.03%	39%
Vornado Realty Trust	VNO, -0.78%	4.15%	6.61%	2.47%	-1%
SL Green Realty Corp.	SLG, +0.15%	4.13%	8.33%	4.20%	-7%
HCP Inc.	US:HCP	3.94%	4.66%	0.72%	52%

Welltower Inc.	WELL, -0.53%	3.79%	4.48%	0.70%	52%
Realty Income Corp.	O, -0.27%	3.42%	3.96%	0.55%	44%
Crown Castle International Corp	CCI, -0.43%	3.40%	4.18%	0.78%	38%
Regency Centers Corp.	REG, -0.19%	3.36%	5.51%	2.15%	15%
Public Storage	PSA, +0.19%	3.33%	4.44%	1.11%	27%
Digital Realty Trust Inc.	DLR, +0.12%	3.20%	4.96%	1.75%	24%
Extra Space Storage Inc.	EXR, -0.99%	3.12%	4.12%	1.00%	39%
Federal Realty Investment Trust	FRT, +0.04%	2.99%	4.49%	1.50%	21%
Boston Properties Inc.	BXP, -0.13%	2.90%	5.14%	2.24%	17%
Apartment Investment and Management Co. Class A	AIV, +0.11%	2.84%	4.69%	1.85%	34%
Mid-America Apartment Communities Inc.	MAA, -0.04%	2.82%	4.55%	1.73%	45%
UDR Inc.	UDR, +0.31%	2.76%	4.08%	1.33%	33%
AvalonBay Communities Inc.	**AVB,** + **0.00%**	2.74%	4.13%	1.39%	32%
Equity Residential	EQR, -0.29%	2.57%	3.88%	1.31%	43%
Alexandria Real Estate Equities Inc.	ARE, +0.99%	2.55%	4.31%	1.77%	34%
Duke Realty Corp.	**DRE,** +0.00%	2.53%	4.08%	1.56%	28%

Essex Property Trust Inc.	ESS, + 0.53%	2.36%	2.90 %	1.54%	40%
Prologis Inc.	PLD, - 1.09%	2.33%	3.60 %	1.27%	48%
Equinix Inc.	EQIX, +2.35%	1.73%	3.85 %	2.13%	41%
American Tower Corp.	AMT, +1.01%	1.59%	3.63 %	2.04%	55%
SBA Communications Corp. Class A	SBAC, +0.01%	0.60%	3.30 %	2.69%	60%
CBRE Group Inc. Class A	CBRE, +1.59%	0.00%	3.31 %	3.81%	32%

Source: Factsheet [6]

Benefits of REITS

REITs have a lot of benefits compared to other types of dividend stocks. They are less volatile and offer a higher yield for investors. More advantages of REIT investment are discussed below.

1.Reliable Business Model

The REIT is based on a simple business model in which companies lease places and receive money in the form of rents. This amount is then distributed among the shareholders as dividends. As per the regulations set by the Generally Accepted Accounting Principles (GAAP), the REITs have to declare their earnings based on each share.

---

[6] https://www.marketwatch.com/story/these-stocks-have-the-highest-dividend-yields-in-the-hot-real-estate-sector-20 9-10-24

2. No Hassles of Property Management

The investors do not have to manage the property as it is the company that does it for them. The investor just needs to invest in an equity and manage dividend payout. Being a landlord is no easy job. You have to be the handyman, the gardener and the 3a.m. problem fixer of anything and everything that can go wrong with the property. REITs offer high yielding returns but without all those hassles. On the upside, you also save money that you may have had to spend on a property manager.

3. Appreciation

The prices of real estate and property entities increase over time. Short term market fluctuations and inflation have a minimum effect upon equity stocks. And in case the real estate business does get affected, it has a history of bouncing back after a certain period of economic upheaval. In this way, the investor not only enjoys higher dividend cash payouts but also appreciation of property overtime.

4. High Distribution

REITs are required by law to distribute 90 percent of their income to the shareholders, and therefore, the dividend cash payout is more than that of other entities. The financial reports are expected to be audited, and therefore a much more transparent process is in place for the shareholders. Moreover, the investment is done on tangible assets and therefore is more secure. It has been reported that REITs have yielded higher returns compared to corporate bonds.

5. Resistance to Challenges

REITs have long survived market conditions, including economic instability and inflation, and have remained consistent in terms of rewarding their shareholders. Because the fact is, no matter how frequently market trends change, people will still need a place to live and workplaces to operate their businesses. As shelter is one of the basic needs of people, it is highly unlikely that the demand for REITs and their returns will ever be negatively affected in the long run.

6. Diversification

REITs encompass a wide range of property investment. An investor can purchase REITs in multiple different areas or types of properties, hence diversifying their portfolio and mitigating risk. This not only encourages investment in various assets but also offsets the risk of investing in one type only.

Disadvantages of Investing in REITS

REITs are a pretty stable form of investment for the most part. But just like any and all businesses, there are specific drawbacks and risks involved too. The following are some of the main risks and disadvantages associated with investing in REITs.

1. Property Tax

One of the biggest disadvantages is that the investors have to pay property tax upon the income they generate as dividend cash payouts. The percentage of property tax can be as high as 25 percent. Another major drawback is that this property tax is subject to change and continues to fluctuate. The municipality may decide to further increase property taxes in order to make up for higher costs, as a result of which, your bottom line or returns can be affected.

High Tax

The dividend cash payouts are considered as ordinary income, and therefore, are taxed as such. The percentage of tax on ordinary income can go up to 15 percent, and therefore the investor has to shell out a considerable amount of money received as dividends.

2. High Management Fee

One thing which an investor must take care of while investing in REITs is that the management fee can be considerably high. An investor must consider it as an additional expense on top of the taxes being paid. Managing properties is no easy task, and while you may not be directly involved, you will still need to take care of the operational costs that come with it.

Types of REIT Investments

Now that you have read the pros and cons of investing in REITs, you should be able to make a better decision as to whether or not they are the right option for you. The fact is, historically, REITs are on top of the best-performing asset classes out there. Investors study the FTSE NAREIT Equity REIT Index to better understand the performance of the real estate market in the United States. The average return was 9.9% during the period between 1990 and 2010. These numbers have only gone higher since then. It was recorded at 11.21% in 2013.

There are 5 types of REITs, and you will need to closely study them before making a decision on which ones of these to include in your portfolio.

Retail REITs

Almost 24% of all REIT investments are in this sector. These include freestanding retail stores as well as shopping malls. These are one of the biggest types of investments in America. There is a fair chance that most of the shopping malls that you must have visited around the country are owned by a REIT. What does that mean for you? It means you can also own a little chunk of that investment. But that's just the tip of the iceberg.

You will need in-depth knowledge of the industry, or the help of a professional retail REIT advisor to get a better understanding of how this operates. In a nutshell, the returns on this income are generated from the rent paid by tenants of the mall.

On the downside, retailers may delay payments due to poor cash flow, or if the mall fails to rent out many of its commercial offerings, then the returns will be negatively impacted. Hence, before you can blindly invest in retail, you will need to ensure that your choice of retail entity is indeed making stable profits. A little look at the entity's balance sheets and debt ratio, and you should be able to get a better understanding of how it is performing.

Residential REITs

These include properties that are built for residential purposes and can include rental apartment buildings. Again, this option, too, has its fair share of risk involved. You will need to find buildings that are located in areas where home affordability is comparatively lower. Doing so would ensure that the chances of the building being rented out all seasons would be higher.

Home affordability is generally lower in larger cities like Los Angeles and New York, as the cost of owning a property is much higher compared to smaller cities. These high costs of ownership drive people to rent out.

Property in rural areas may offer higher REIT returns in order to lure investors in, but the chances of the market fluctuating or the property remaining vacant are much higher compared to residential complexes in big cities.

Big cities are populated enough to make it easier to find tenants all year round. The declining vacancy rates and an increase in rents in recent times are proof enough that residential REITs, when invested incorrectly, can yield stable and sustainable returns.

Healthcare REITs

As the name suggests, these include the real estate of medical centers, hospitals, retirement homes, and nursing facilities. The success of investing in this type of REIT mainly depends on healthcare funding as most of the returns will be generated from Medicaid and Medicare reimbursements, occupancy fees, and private pay.

Office REITs

This is an uncommon option, but one that can yield the right returns when invested incorrectly. Office REITs generate cash flow by receiving rental income from office tenants. The main advantage of this type of structure is that once occupied; there are relatively lower chances of an office relocating elsewhere anytime soon. Of course, this isn't a hard and fast rule, but the chances are slimmer, hence leading to a more stable stream of income. Again, you will have to do in-depth research on office vacancy rates, economic conditions, and rising job markets in order to invest wisely and profitably.

Mortgage REITs

This is a lesser-known and even lesser employed option. Only 10% of all REIT investments consist of a mortgage. This is the only REIT option that profits from a mortgage rather than equity. At first glance, one might think it is a foolproof option since mortgages will need to be paid off regularly; hence there'd be lesser chances of dividend fluctuation. However, in cases of higher interest rates, the mortgage REIT book value will be lower, causing the stock prices to take a plunge too.

CHAPTER 5

BUILDING YOUR EARLY RETIREMENT PORTFOLIO

Investing in dividend stocks is no different than looking for a house to buy. As an investor, you would like to gain maximum advantage and reward out of your investment while minimizing the associated risks. In the same way, most people, especially nearing their retirement period, are on a lookout for investment plans that can fulfill their financial requirements and become a regular source of income.

Investors building retirement portfolios usually look at options like investing in bonds, real estate, dividends, etc. At the heart of all of these options is to make decisions that will be lower risk, increase profits, and be able to create a steady stream of income come retirement.

Risk tolerance is another important factor. Every investor has a different tolerance to risk. While some are risk-takers, others are more conservative or cautious in nature. Investment decisions also factor in other considerations like age, financial goals, and personal preferences.

Factors to Consider

Your Age

You can take higher risks at a younger age since you'll have time to rectify or reap from your decisions at a later stage. For instance, say you have invested in real estate when the economy isn't doing so well. But the fact is you will be gaining equity. Say you have 30 years to retirement, there is a fair chance the real estate market will go uphill at some point, and you can cash out your investment and make better decisions with your investment.

Your Goals

In order to prepare for the future, you need to know what you would like it to look like. You would be better able to plan your investments once you have planned your future. For instance, if you'd like to retire early, own your home by that time, and have a diversified investment portfolio by then, then you'd likely need to invest a larger chunk of your monthly income in doing so.

However, if you are just looking for steady cash to help maintain your simple lifestyle come late retirement, then the chances are you could get away with only investing a little each month.

Your Risk Tolerance

Some people are risk-takers, whereas others are faint-hearted. For an investor in the second category, it is important to invest in low-risk options.

Your Monthly Revenue

Investment decisions depend upon wealth as well. A person willing to invest may have bills and expenses to cover, and therefore, he must consider playing it safe. If the amount of wealth is insufficient, perhaps the best way to remain safe is to avoid making a high level of investments.

Thoughts Surrounding Retirement

In a highly volatile and unpredictable global and economic landscape, people have started to rely on secondary income options. Previously, people would not have worried much about investing at a younger age, and retirees would have plenty of options to choose from. However, the situation has changed, and people have begun to think about effective retirement investment plans way ahead of time. Some of the questions that an individual has in mind regarding retirement are:

- How much should I save now to live a comfortable life post-retirement?

- How can I make my retirement earnings last?

- How much should I save every month from arriving at a reasonable amount to cover retirement needs?

- What are the ways in which I can earn a reasonable and consistent income on my savings?

With so many questions in mind, an investor may seek answers in order to consider an efficient and effective dividend investment strategy that could yield a regular income stream. Investing in stocks is a process and consists of various steps and some important factors to be considered. The following sections will provide an in-depth analysis of the same and facilitate the retirees or near-to-retirement employees with ample information to make rational decisions.

The Right Time to Invest

The right time to invest is as early as possible, probably as soon as you finish school. Even small investments will keep earning a small but steady income and lead to compounding. Imagine if you begin saving $ 1,000 every year beginning at the age of 26 with an annual return ration of 7 percent. Within the next ten years, your savings could increase and compound many times. The earlier you invest, the higher returns you'd generate come retirement. Perhaps you may even be able to retire early!

Knowing the Right Mix

Stocks, bonds, and mutual funds are some of the options an investor can consider to have a retirement-based investment plan. Ideally, your portfolio should consist of a mix of stocks and dividends from different industries and sectors. Mutual funds and bonds are much riskier in the sense that economic volatility may impact the return significantly. However, dividend investment can help counter the risk provided the investment is made in the right companies.

Determine How Much You Want to Make?

The investor portfolio depends greatly on how much money he wants to make. This is where you determine your short- and long-term goals. Any form of investing without a plan has a very lower chances of success. So you would really need to have a plan. Know how much you want to make so that you will be able to lead the lifestyle you have imagined and planned for yourself. Say you would like to generate a cash flow of $5000 per month, then you'd need to plan and invest accordingly. The following is everything you need to know on how to make targeted calculations for dividend investments:

Calculating Dividend Yield and Ratio

The dividend yield is derived by applying a simple formula of dividing the per-share dividend payout by the current market value of the share. It is the amount that has been paid by the companies to its shareholders. The simple formula to calculate dividend yield is as follows:

Dividend Yield = Dividend per share / Market value per share

For instance, the trading value of the stocks for company XYZ is $45. This results in a quarterly payout dividend of $0.30 per share. Keeping in view these values, the dividend yield would be 2.7%. The dividend yield ratio must be calculated for the companies within the same industry. The level of dividend yield is dependent upon the type of industry as well and can be described in the following manner:

- ❖ Utilities 3.96%

- ❖ Healthcare industry 2.28 %

- ❖ Financial services 4.17 %

- ❖ Technology industry 3.1 %

- ❖ Materials industry 4.8%

How to Interpret the Dividend Yield Formula

The dividend yield formula is essential to provide an insight into the cash flow pertaining to the investment in the company stock. The company with a higher dividend yield does not always refer to the potential for future growth. For instance, a company that has already reached the maturity stage would have no advantage in further investing, and therefore it may payout significantly to its stockholders. There are no criteria to judge how good or bad a company is by applying the dividend yield formula, but it must be considered while taking investment decisions.

Value Trap

The company with higher yields means that the amount which it is given out to the stockholders is capital that it is not reinvesting for its growth. But this is not always the case as high dividend yield may also mean that the stock price is decreasing. This situation is known as a value trap, so the investor needs to conduct thorough research on reasons for such unusual high returns. Perhaps the falling price of stocks may reveal that the company is going through a financial crisis.

Not all companies with higher yield are bad

Some of the higher yields are pertaining to the type of industry. For example, REITs and MLPs have a significantly higher dividend yield because the state laws make it necessary for these companies to share a significant amount of their earnings with the stockholders.

But wait....

Some companies may also show higher yields to attract investors and then not deliver what they promised. Ideally, the investor must conduct an analysis of the growth rate history of the company to make better decisions.

Dividend Payout Ratio (DPR)

The term refers to the total amount that a company shares with its shareholders after receiving the corporate earnings. There are various formulas to calculate the dividend payout ratio.

DPR = amount of dividends / company's earnings

DPR = 1 – Retention ratio

Example

For instance, the company XYZ has reported its annual earnings of $100,000. The same year the company has paid out $20,000 as dividends to the shareholders. Therefore, the dividend payout ratio would be:

DPR= 20,000 / 100,000 = 20 %

According to this example, 20 % is the dividend payout ratio that the company has distributed among its shareholders, whereas the remaining 80 % is the amount that the company retains for the growth of its business and is known as retained earnings.

Net Income: $ 20,000

Retained earnings: $ 15,000

Dividend payout: $ 5,000

How to Interpret the DPR

The DPR is an important consideration for investors to determine whether a said investment is worth the time. Dividend and capital gains are two sources from which investors receive their returns.

A lower percentage of DPR refers to the fact that the company is re-investing more money into the business for further expansion. This is a suitable option for individuals looking for an increase in stock value instead of dividend payout. This is a suitable option to invest in retirement plans.

The higher level of DPR depicts exactly the opposite. It means that the company is giving out a large number of its earnings to the shareholders while retaining a lesser amount for reinvesting. Such companies attract investors that are on the lookout for dividend income rather than an increase in share price over the years.

The Sustainability Factors

The dividend payout ratio is also essential to assess the sustainability level of the dividend. It is quite rare that the companies decrease the payout ratio because that would drive the stock price down. During an economic recession, the company may be forced to reduce the DPR, especially when it has been paying more than a hundred percent to its shareholders. The company would like to retain the percentage of its earnings to mitigate the risks associated with the economic slowdown. Therefore, the company must consider the expectations of the investors and the future outcome of fluctuating stock prices while setting the DPR.

Dividend Yield vs. Dividend Payout Ratio

Both of these terms are used to measure the dividends. However, the DPR refers to the amount that the company pays as dividends to the shareholders, whereas dividend yield refers to the rate of return. The DPR is believed to be a better indicator of a company's performance as it is directly linked to the cash flow. In terms of dividend yield, it is the percentage of dividend payout by the company over a year. While the DPR is shown as a dollar amount, the dividend yield is expressed in the form of a percentage.

Strategies for Investing Based on Dividend Yields

The Relative Dividend Yields

This strategy was developed by Anthony Spare in the 1960s, the co-founder of Spare, Kaplan, Bischel & Associates, and uses the value equity strategy to focus upon the stocks that have a relatively higher dividend yield. Spare advises the investors to pay attention to these stocks although this strategy is not suitable for the investor seeking short term rewards because it is a long-term strategy stretching up on up to 5 years and is not dependent upon the assessment of past performance or future growth opportunities.

According to this strategy, investors must opt for investing in bigger companies and then let their investments mature because such companies have successfully maintained their cash flow, even during the turbulent economic situations, and therefore, are stable enough to offer optimum yields.

This strategy suggests that the stocks must be bought when their yield is 50% higher as compared to the market. Also, it pertains to less volatility because the investors hold the stocks for longer periods and considered the mature and well-established companies that have undergone all sorts of economic conditions.

The Geraldine Weiss Strategy

Known as the Grande Dame of Dividends, the leading expert of dividend investment Geraldine Weiss suggests investors buy the stocks when the yields are high and sell them at their extreme lows. The Weiss approach pertains to the blue-chip stocks and is rather a conservative strategy that uses the dividend yield asset tool to measure the value of the stocks. By doing so, an investor can know about the direction of the market as well as the value of the company.

The Dogs of the Dow

The strategy was developed by Michael O'Higgins in 1991 and referred to the concept that the dividend yield of a stock is inversely proportional to the share price. In other words, the stock dividend yield increases as the price of the share drops.

According to this strategy, the investors must consider investing in the 10 highest dividend-yielding stocks and rebalancing it every year. The strategy is that well-established companies do not fluctuate their dividend payouts according to the market fluctuations. Please note that the companies with the highest dividend yields have apparently reached the bottom of the business cycle, and therefore, the price of the stocks will increase at an exponential rate.

The Dividend Achiever List

This strategy has a simple approach as it refers to the well-established and performance-oriented companies that have a proven track record of successful business and dividend growth every year. In order to make its way into the dividend achievers index, the company must have at least 10 years of consecutive growth and must be listed on one of the well-established stock exchanges. Currently, the dividend achiever list consists of over 250 companies as compared to 19 in the Dividend King Lost and 52 in the Dividend Aristocrats list. Below is the list of Dividend Achievers for the year 2019

Holdings Ticker	Name	Sector
VZ	Verizon Communications Inc	Communication Services
T	AT&T Inc	Communication Services
CMCSA	Comcast Corp	Communication Services
TDS	Telephone & Data Systems Inc	Communication Services
MDP	Meredith Corp	Communication Services
JW/A	John Wiley & Sons Inc	Communication Services
MCD	McDonald's Corp	Consumer Discretionary
NKE	NIKE Inc	Consumer Discretionary
LOW	Lowe's Cos Inc	Consumer Discretionary
TJX	TJX Cos Inc/The	Consumer Discretionary
TGT	Target Corp	Consumer Discretionary
ROST	Ross Stores Inc	Consumer Discretionary
VFC	VF Corp	Consumer Discretionary
BBY	Best Buy Co Inc	Consumer Discretionary
GPC	Genuine Parts Co	Consumer Discretionary

TIF	Tiffany & Co	Consumer Discretionary
HAS	Hasbro Inc	Consumer Discretionary
COLM	Columbia Sportswear Co	Consumer Discretionary
PII	Polaris Industries Inc	Consumer Discretionary
LEG	Leggett & Platt Inc	Consumer Discretionary
WSM	Williams-Sonoma Inc	Consumer Discretionary
CBRL	Cracker Barrel Old Country Store Inc	Consumer Discretionary
AAN	Aaron's Inc	Consumer Discretionary
MNRO	Monro Inc	Consumer Discretionary
ISCA	International Speedway Corp	Consumer Discretionary
WMT	Walmart Inc	Consumer Staples
PG	Procter & Gamble Co/The	Consumer Staples
KO	Coca-Cola Co/The	Consumer Staples
PEP	PepsiCo Inc	Consumer Staples
PM	Philip Morris International Inc	Consumer Staples
COST	Costco Wholesale Corp	Consumer Staples
MO	Altria Group Inc	Consumer Staples
CL	Colgate-Palmolive Co	Consumer Staples
WBA	Walgreens Boots Alliance Inc	Consumer Staples
KMB	Kimberly-Clark Corp	Consumer Staples
SYY	Sysco Corp	Consumer Staples
GIS	General Mills Inc	Consumer Staples
ADM	Archer-Daniels-Midland Co	Consumer Staples
HRL	Hormel Foods Corp	Consumer Staples
K	Kellogg Co	Consumer Staples
CLX	Clorox Co/The	Consumer Staples

KR	Kroger Co/The	Consumer Staples
MKC	McCormick & Co Inc/MD	Consumer Staples
CHD	Church & Dwight Co Inc	Consumer Staples
BF/B	Brown-Forman Corp	Consumer Staples
SJM	JM Smucker Co/The	Consumer Staples
BG	Bunge Ltd	Consumer Staples
CASY	Casey's General Stores Inc	Consumer Staples
FLO	Flowers Foods Inc	Consumer Staples
LANC	Lancaster Colony Corp	Consumer Staples
JJSF	J&J Snack Foods Corp	Consumer Staples
NUS	Nu Skin Enterprises Inc	Consumer Staples
TR	Tootsie Roll Industries Inc	Consumer Staples
VGR	Vector Group Ltd	Consumer Staples
UVV	Universal Corp/VA	Consumer Staples
ANDE	Andersons Inc/The	Consumer Staples
XOM	Exxon Mobil Corp	Energy
CVX	Chevron Corp	Energy
EPD	Enterprise Products Partners LP	Energy
OXY	Occidental Petroleum Corp	Energy
ET	Energy Transfer LP	Energy
OKE	ONEOK Inc	Energy
MMP	Magellan Midstream Partners LP	Energy
HP	Helmerich & Payne Inc	Energy
HEP	Holly Energy Partners LP	Energy
CB	Chubb Ltd	Financials
SPGI	S&P Global Inc	Financials
PRU	Prudential Financial Inc	Financials

AFL	Aflac Inc	Financials
TRV	Travelers Cos Inc/The	Financials
TROW	T Rowe Price Group Inc	Financials
AMP	Ameriprise Financial Inc	Financials
BEN	Franklin Resources Inc	Financials
PFG	Principal Financial Group Inc	Financials
CINF	Cincinnati Financial Corp	Financials
WRB	WR Berkley Corp	Financials
FDS	FactSet Research Systems Inc	Financials
TMK	Torchmark Corp	Financials
AFG	American Financial Group Inc/OH	Financials
SEIC	SEI Investments Co	Financials
BRO	Brown & Brown Inc	Financials
IVZ	Invesco Ltd	Financials
ERIE	Erie Indemnity Co	Financials
UNM	Unum Group	Financials
CBSH	Commerce Bancshares Inc/MO	Financials
CFR	Cullen/Frost Bankers Inc	Financials
PBCT	People's United Financial Inc	Financials
ORI	Old Republic International Corp	Financials
RNR	Renaissance Re Holdings Ltd	Financials
AIZ	Assurant Inc	Financials
BOKF	BOK Financial Corp	Financials
PB	Prosperity Bancshares Inc	Financials
EV	Eaton Vance Corp	Financials

THG	Hanover Insurance Group Inc/The	Financials
AXS	Axis Capital Holdings Ltd	Financials
LAZ	Lazard Ltd	Financials
UBSI	United Bankshares Inc/WV	Financials
OZK	Bank OZK	Financials
EVR	Evercore Inc	Financials
UMBF	UMB Financial Corp	Financials
RLI	RLI Corp	Financials
CBU	Community Bank System Inc	Financials
MCY	Mercury General Corp	Financials
AEL	American Equity Investment Life Holding Co	Financials
BANF	BancFirst Corp	Financials
WABC	Westamerica Bancorporation	Financials
TMP	Tompkins Financial Corp	Financials
SRCE	1st Source Corp	Financials
SBSI	Southside Bancshares Inc	Financials
CTBI	Community Trust Bancorp Inc	Financials
BMRC	Bank of Marin Bancorp	Financials
FLIC	First of Long Island Corp/The	Financials
WHG	Westwood Holdings Group Inc	Financials
JNJ	Johnson & Johnson	Health Care
ABT	Abbott Laboratories	Health Care
MDT	Medtronic PLC	Health Care
SYK	Stryker Corp	Health Care

BDX	Becton Dickinson and Co	Health Care
MCK	McKesson Corp	Health Care
ABC	AmerisourceBergen Corp	Health Care
CAH	Cardinal Health Inc	Health Care
WST	West Pharmaceutical Services Inc	Health Care
PRGO	Perrigo Co PLC	Health Care
CHE	Chemed Corp	Health Care
ENSG	Ensign Group Inc/The	Health Care
ATRI	Atrion Corp	Health Care
NHC	National HealthCare Corp	Health Care
MMM	3M Co	Industrials
UNP	Union Pacific Corp	Industrials
UTX	United Technologies Corp	Industrials
LMT	Lockheed Martin Corp	Industrials
CAT	Caterpillar Inc	Industrials
CSX	CSX Corp	Industrials
RTN	Raytheon Co	Industrials
FDX	FedEx Corp	Industrials
ITW	Illinois Tool Works Inc	Industrials
GD	General Dynamics Corp	Industrials
NOC	Northrop Grumman Corp	Industrials
EMR	Emerson Electric Co	Industrials
WM	Waste Management Inc	Industrials
ROP	Roper Technologies Inc	Industrials
RSG	Republic Services Inc	Industrials
CMI	Cummins Inc	Industrials
SWK	Stanley Black & Decker Inc	Industrials
CTAS	Cintas Corp	Industrials

HRS	Harris Corp	Industrials
FAST	Fastenal Co	Industrials
GWW	WW Grainger Inc	Industrials
DOV	Dover Corp	Industrials
ROL	Rollins Inc	Industrials
EXPD	Expeditors International of Washington Inc	Industrials
CHRW	CH Robinson Worldwide Inc	Industrials
JBHT	JB Hunt Transport Services Inc	Industrials
GGG	Graco Inc	Industrials
NDSN	Nordson Corp	Industrials
RHI	Robert Half International Inc	Industrials
AOS	AO Smith Corp	Industrials
TTC	Toro Co/The	Industrials
CSL	Carlisle Cos Inc	Industrials
HUBB	Hubbell Inc	Industrials
DCI	Donaldson Co Inc	Industrials
LECO	Lincoln Electric Holdings Inc	Industrials
ITT	ITT Inc	Industrials
HEI	HEICO Corp	Industrials
MSA	MSA Safety Inc	Industrials
MSM	MSC Industrial Direct Co Inc	Industrials
RBC	Regal Beloit Corp	Industrials
R	Ryder System Inc	Industrials
HI	Hillenbrand Inc	Industrials
HCSG	Healthcare Services Group Inc	Industrials

ABM	ABM Industries Inc	Industrials
BRC	Brady Corp	Industrials
FELE	Franklin Electric Co Inc	Industrials
MGRC	McGrath RentCorp	Industrials
MATW	Matthews International Corp	Industrials
TNC	Tennant Co	Industrials
LNN	Lindsay Corp	Industrials
GRC	Gorman-Rupp Co/The	Industrials
MSFT	Microsoft Corp	Information Technology
V	Visa Inc	Information Technology
IBM	International Business Machines Corp	Information Technology
ACN	Accenture PLC	Information Technology
TXN	Texas Instruments Inc	Information Technology
ADP	Automatic Data Processing Inc	Information Technology
QCOM	QUALCOMM Inc	Information Technology
ADI	Analog Devices Inc	Information Technology
XLNX	Xilinx Inc	Information Technology
MCHP	Microchip Technology Inc	Information Technology
MXIM	Maxim Integrated Products Inc	Information Technology
BR	Broadridge Financial Solutions Inc	Information Technology
JKHY	Jack Henry & Associates Inc	Information Technology
BMI	Badger Meter Inc	Information Technology
CASS	Cass Information Systems Inc	Information Technology
ECL	Ecolab Inc	Materials
APD	Air Products & Chemicals Inc	Materials

SHW	Sherwin-Williams Co/The	Materials
PPG	PPG Industries Inc	Materials
NUE	Nucor Corp	Materials
IFF	International Flavors & Fragrances Inc	Materials
WLK	Westlake Chemical Corp	Materials
HoldingsTicker	Name	Sector
ALB	Albemarle Corp	Materials
RPM	RPM International Inc	Materials
ATR	AptarGroup Inc	Materials
SON	Sonoco Products Co	Materials
RGLD	Royal Gold Inc	Materials
SLGN	Silgan Holdings Inc	Materials
BCPC	Balchem Corp	Materials
SXT	Sensient Technologies Corp	Materials
KWR	Quaker Chemical Corp	Materials
FUL	HB Fuller Co	Materials
SCL	Stepan Co	Materials
HWKN	Hawkins Inc	Materials
DLR	Digital Realty Trust Inc	Real Estate
O	Realty Income Corp	Real Estate
ESS	Essex Property Trust Inc	Real Estate
WPC	WP Carey Inc	Real Estate
ELS	Equity LifeStyle Properties Inc	Real Estate
FRT	Federal Realty Investment Trust	Real Estate
NNN	National Retail Properties Inc	Real Estate

OHI	Omega Healthcare Investors Inc	Real Estate
NHI	National Health Investors Inc	Real Estate
SKT	Tanger Factory Outlet Centers Inc	Real Estate
UHT	Universal Health Realty Income Trust	Real Estate
UBA	Urstadt Biddle Properties Inc	Real Estate
NEE	NextEra Energy Inc	Utilities
DUK	Duke Energy Corp	Utilities
D	Dominion Energy Inc	Utilities
SO	Southern Co/The	Utilities
XEL	Xcel Energy Inc	Utilities
ED	Consolidated Edison Inc	Utilities
WEC	WEC Energy Group Inc	Utilities
PPL	PPL Corp	Utilities
ES	Eversource Energy	Utilities
EIX	Edison International	Utilities
AWK	American Water Works Co Inc	Utilities
CMS	CMS Energy Corp	Utilities
CNP	CenterPoint Energy Inc	Utilities
EVRG	Evergy Inc	Utilities
ATO	Atmos Energy Corp	Utilities
BIP	Brookfield Infrastructure Partners LP	Utilities
LNT	Alliant Energy Corp	Utilities
UGI	UGI Corp	Utilities
OGE	OGE Energy Corp	Utilities
WTR	Aqua America Inc	Utilities

NFG	National Fuel Gas Co	Utilities
MDU	MDU Resources Group Inc	Utilities
POR	Portland General Electric Co	Utilities
SWX	Southwest Gas Holdings Inc	Utilities
BKH	Black Hills Corp	Utilities
NJR	New Jersey Resources Corp	Utilities
SR	Spire Inc	Utilities
NWE	NorthWestern Corp	Utilities
APU	AmeriGas Partners LP	Utilities
SJI	South Jersey Industries Inc	Utilities
AWR	American States Water Co	Utilities
CWT	California Water Service Group	Utilities
MGEE	MGE Energy Inc	Utilities
NWN	Northwest Natural Holding Co	Utilities
SJW	SJW Group	Utilities
CPK	Chesapeake Utilities Corp	Utilities
MSEX	Middlesex Water Co	Utilities

When Do You Want to Retire?

Living off dividends depends significantly on when you want to retire as well as the lifestyle which you look forward to maintaining. For instance, an individual may have a goal to retire in his 50s and spend his time traveling around the world. This may differ for another investor that is looking forward to retiring at the standard age and wants a steady flow of income post-retirement to cover expenses. Both of these retirement plans cater to different amounts of expected income, hence a different percentage of savings and investments.

For someone wanting to retire early, they'd need to invest a higher percentage of their income on a monthly basis compared to someone looking for just a little cushion apart from their pension.

The current generation is expected to be aggressively invested in passive sources of income and have a consistent retirement plan in place. However, it is suggested that not more than 50 percent of the savings must be invested in stocks.

Four Percent Rule of Retirement

This rule sets a limit on how much a retiree should ideally withdraw from their retirement account every passing year. This rule helps maintain balance with investment and income stream for retirees. 4% withdrawal rate is considered by experts to be safe and sufficient to long term investment, and savings plans as the withdrawal will likely only consist of interest and dividends rather than the initial investment amount that can continue to grow.

Words of Caution

Although the 4 percent rule has demonstrated success in the past since the economic situation has become quite volatile, the 4 percent rule cannot be considered as an ultimate or foolproof solution. This rule also does not include taxation bills and payments, leading to higher costs.

CHAPTER 6

TAX BENEFITS FROM DIVIDEND INVESTING

What are Qualified Dividends?

When an investor buys stocks, he is liable to pay taxes on them. One can either opt for ordinary or qualified taxes. The latter is better as the percentage is lower compared to that of ordinary taxes. Qualified dividends must be issued by companies that are under US possession or listed in the major US exchange. Moreover, the investor must have owned the stocks for more than 60 days before the ex-dividend date. Dividends on entities such as bank deposits, gain distributions, tax-exempt corporations, or are held by the Employee Stock Ownership Plan and do not fall under qualified dividends.

Dividend Taxes

The difference between qualified and non-qualified dividends is significant when it comes to being taxed. The qualified dividends have much less tax imposed as

114

compared to the ordinary or non-qualified. For instance, if an investor owns stocks worth $500,000 on which he receives an annual income of $20,000 and the average yield is reported at 4 percent annually.

With respect to the qualified dividend policy, the investor will be taxed at $3,000, whereas ordinary dividend policy would make him pay around $5,600 in taxes, and therefore, significantly reducing the amount the investor will receive as an income. Below is the comparison of both types of dividends with respect to the charged tax rates.

Qualified Dividend Tax Rate	Ordinary Income Tax Rate
0 %	10%
0 %	15%
15%	25%
15%	28%
15%	33%
15%	35%
20%	39.6%

Taxes on qualified dividends have been 0 percent, 15 percent and 20 percent depending upon the income level of the investor. The only difference that has been reported in the policy is with respect to the long-term gains that are now independent of the income brackets.

As for the 2020, the eligibility criteria for taxation on qualified dividends are as below:

0 Percent Tax Bracket	15 Percent Tax Bracket	20 Percent Tax Bracket
The investor is married, maintains a joint return with spouse and has an income of USD 80,000 or below.	Income for single investors is USD 441,450	The investors eligible for 20 percent tax are the ones with 15 percent increased threshold of income.
If investor is single and income is USD 40,000 or below	Married investors with joint returns must have income of USD 496,600	
If the investor is the head of the household and income level is USD 53,600 or below.	Household heads accounting for income of USD 469,050	

Dividend Taxation Policies as Per Country

In most countries the state imposes corporate tax on the earnings of a company. In the case of the dividend payout, the amount is considered as an income for the shareholder but not an expense for the company. But it varies from country to country. Here is an overview of taxation policies of countries with the most influential stock markets.

USA and Canada

In the US and Canada, the tax rate on dividend payout is comparatively less because it is already paid by the company in the form of corporate tax.

United Kingdom

In the UK a company releases the dividend payout after paying the corporate tax which has witnessed variations from 20 % to 19% in 2017. The shareholders are expected to pay tax on the dividend income of 7.5% for basic ratepayers. The high taxpayers are charged 32.5% whereas the additional ratepayers have to shell out 38.1%. The income amount received above £2,000 is taxed and collected through personal tax returns.

India

In India, the companies have to pay corporate dividend tax on top of the income tax. In this case the investor does not have to pay tax on his dividend income provided that the amount remains lower than INR 1000, 000 over which the shareholder is liable to pay 10% of dividend tax.

Australia and New Zealand

Countries including New Zealand and Australia have the option of attaching imputation credits to the dividend and this is known as the dividend imputation system. According to the system, $1 paid by the company in tax counts as one imputed credit. This saves the shareholder from paying double taxation on the companies earning.

CHAPTER 7

BUILDING A STELLAR PORTFOLIO

You must have heard the importance of building an investment portfolio again and again. Anyone and everyone who knows anything about stock and dividend investments knows the importance of a diversified portfolio. But what does that really mean? It is a common misconception that a portfolio consists of shares in multiple different stocks rather than investing in just one company.

Sure, it is the gist of it, but a good, profitable and somewhat foolproof portfolio is one that is built on different TYPES of stocks and their payout methods among other important considerations we will be discussing in-depth in this section.

There are a lot of other factors to consider while building the portfolio such as assessing the risk ratio and looking out for the market conditions.

Why You Shouldn't Just Randomly Invest in Different Companies

Markets are extremely unpredictable. Even a controversial speech by the US President has proven to affect stock markets greatly. Regardless of how stable a company is, or how well a specific industry has been performing in recent times, the stock market remains dangerously unpredictable. From an incompetent CEO to a problem with the labor union, anything can shake up the company's stocks by large margins.

Even if you invest in a number of different companies, similar factors make random investments risky. Hence, it is strongly advised to not put all your eggs in one basket! Not to say there is a surefire or fail-proof way to build a portfolio, but as an investor with hefty amounts of money on the line, it is up to you to mitigate all risks to the minimum.

Lehman Brothers is a great example of how a successful, and apparently stable company came crashing down due to a mortgage crisis back in 2008, leaving all its shareholders hanging out to dry.

If your portfolio is diversified, you are likely to escape a few upheavals. But the secret is to make sure that diversity must reflect in the *types of industry* rather than just companies.

For instance, a drop-in *oil gas* business can still yield you with a better dividend payout from consumer staples. Considering the history of the US market, it is likely to show growth in the future as well and diversified portfolio will prevent you from bearing hefty losses. A typical diverse portfolio would look like the table below:

Dividend Stock	Sector	Yield
Disney	Consumer discretionary	1.6%
Procter & Gamble	Consumer Staples	3.7%
ExxonMobil	Energy	4%
JPMorgan Chase	Financials	2.1%
Johnson & Johnson	Healthcare	2.9%
Boeing	Industrials	2%
DowDuPont	Materials	2.3%
Simon Property Group	Real estate	4.6%
Apple	Technology	1.6%
Duke Energy	Utilities	4.5%
	Average	3%

DATA SOURCE: GOOGLE FINANCE

With thousands of companies doing well in the market, how is one supposed to select the appropriate ones? The selection of companies is an important part of building a portfolio because your earnings will highly depend upon them. It is also not possible to buy shares for every company but just selects a few based on their past performance and growth percentage. But remember, an insufficient and ineffective portfolio can increase the risk rather than avert it, so you had better be thorough with your research.

Reasons for Investing in Dividend Stock Portfolio

Of course, the primary reason for investors to invest in dividend stocks is its stability, which is more reliable compared to stock prices. During the economic recession of 2008, more than 35% of the S&P 500 stock prices lost their value, but the dividend payout was actually more during this time. An exception was witnessed during the immense recession in 2009 when the S&P 500 companies reduced the dividend payout, but even then, it was a good amount at 20%. The dividend payout again increased in the following years and reached the maximum in 2011.

Imagine an investor who had bought several stocks in 1970 would have received a significant dividend payout a few decades later. Interestingly, as inflation increased by up to 700% during those decades, the dividend payout increased by up to 2,400%.

Similarly, the inflation after 2000 increased by up to 46%, whereas the dividend payout by the S&P 500 companies has risen to more than 200%. Needless to say, the yields from having a diversified portfolio are a great weather shield for all economic seasons.

Consider the Risk Factors

When building a portfolio, make sure you consider all the risk factors involved. For instance, nobody could have predicted the oil and gas industry taking a downward turn. But a few acts of terrorism and political turmoil around the globe and the tables turned quite aggressively. To date, this specific industry remains under the crutches of political disturbance.

Hence, it is extremely important that you understand the current economic and political conditions, not just in your country but across the globe before you make purchasing decisions.

Follow investment mentors and advisors to understand better how these conditions can impact your investments.

Number of Stocks

Most investors would not believe this, but having future stocks can actually be healthy for the dividend portfolio. According to the American Association of Individual Investors (AAII), the volatility of holding single stock is 30% more as compared to a diversified portfolio.

There are certain rules to follow, which may not guarantee higher yields but will decrease the risk factors associated with such investments.

- Investment in 400 stocks can reduce the diversifiable risk by approximately 95%.

- Investment in a hundred stocks can reduce the diversifiable risk by 90%.

- Investing in 25 stocks can reduce diversifiable risk by approximately 80%.

Holding stocks lower than 50 can significantly reduce the trading cost and save the time of investors that could otherwise be spent researching various companies. Various studies conducted in this regard have reported that a safe bet would be to invest in around 25 to 100 stocks.

Financial Leverage

Financial leverage is one of the significant risk factors to consider while investing in dividend stocks. If a company has more debts, the stocks will greatly fluctuate during volatile business and/or economic conditions.

Increased interest rates are not favorable for smaller but highly levered companies because, in such situations, the credit conditions tighten as well. Therefore, it is important to consider the credit value of the company in which the investor is interested in investing because these stocks are likely going to have a high volatility level.

Considering the Industry Diversification

As highlighted before, it is highly recommended that an investor opts for a wide range of industries when building a portfolio. Ideally, you shouldn't invest more than 25% in one specific industry.

It can be quite tempting for investors to opt for a specific industry that has been yielding higher returns, or because they are interested/knowledgeable of a specific industry. But this exposes the investments to higher risks compared to investments in diversified industries.

There are certain industries, like consumer staples, that are relatively turmoil proof, but even they are exposed to various risks and thus shouldn't be entirely relied upon.

Does Size Matter?

Of course, it does. For bigger companies, there are more trading opportunities as a number of buyers and sellers are significant as compared to the companies with smaller market caps. Such companies have fewer buyers and sellers with a tighter liquidity ratio. It is difficult for smaller companies to match the price difference that bigger companies can unwaveringly offer.

It is highly suggested against investing significantly in companies with small-cap stocks because those are highly likely to outperform or underperform and have a higher volatility rate. For example, while trading stocks for Microsoft, the seller can have the advantage of having a large number of buyers that are willing to pay the sellers price.

For instance, as compared to S&P 500 and Dow Jones, Russell 2000 showed high volatility due to relatively smaller cap stocks. By investing in bigger and well-known companies, an investor can relax even during economic turbulence as such companies have a higher rate of recovery.

Standard Deviation from 1989 - 2017		
Dow Jones	S&P 500	Russell 2000
14.8%	16.8%	18.5%

Understanding the Beta

The aforementioned risk factors are significant to be considered, but there is another factor as well known as the beta or price volatility, and it comes into play in the long-term holding time frame in case you are looking for significant growth in the dividend portfolio.

The price for the literacy of stocks is also significantly influenced by the four factors mentioned above. However, it must also be considered that a company that has shown a low beta trend in the past is not likely to have the same in the coming years, and that makes beta a backward-looking trend.

Know your Personal Goals

As you keep the aforementioned factors in mind, it is also essential for you to define your goals. Considered asking yourself the following questions:

- Why are you planning on investing?

- How much can you invest?

- How much risk are you willing to take and tolerate?

- Are you investing to receive regular income after your retirement?

- For how long are you willing to commit to the investment?

Once you have clarity about these factors, it will be easier for you to build your portfolio using your choice of tool.

Tools for Dividend

The advancement in technology, especially with respect to finances and the stock market, means various software and tools are in place for the new as well as experienced investors. There are many assistive tools, apps, and software available that can truly help investors make better investing decisions as well as keep track of their investments. However, not all of these assistive tools are as supportive and as helpful as one might expect them to be. Purchasing the right software or app is an important investment. The following are some important considerations when searching for the right technological support.

- It must be able to show details of all your dividend investments individually as well as an overview.

- We should be able to notify you via email or push notifications regarding any activity in relation to your dividend investments.

- Provides investor access to various dividend related published reports.

- Research and suggest investment-worthy stocks on a regular basis.

- Prevent the investor from receiving dividend cuts by providing a safe score system.

- It provides the option to export the portfolio in two spreadsheets for later analysis.

Below is a sample of what your dividend analysis tool or software display should look like.

Ticker	Shares	Price	% of Portfolio	Gain or Loss (%)	Dividend Yield	Yield on Cost	Dividend Safety	Dividend Growth	Annual Income
+ New Holdings Import ▾			37 holdings					Columns ▾	⬇ Export
ABBV	225	$68.25 ▾ 0.1%	4.1%	42.7%	6.27%	9.26%	50	50% last year Very Fast	$963
ARCC	600	$18.18 ▴ 0.2%	2.9%	5.2%	8.80%	9.63%	59	4% this year Slow	$960
BUD	100	$89.34 ▴ 1.2%	2.4%	-18.0%	1.69%	1.38%	44	-53% last year Very Slow	$151
BXMT	500	$35.80 ▴ 0.4%	4.8%	30.3%	6.93%	9.03%	27	0% last year Very Slow	$1,240

Dividend Screening

To maintain a stellar dividend investment portfolio, screening of dividend stocks is an important step. There are various tools and techniques available in this regard. With the help of these tools, investors can screen equities by a selection of characteristics including annual dividend and sector rating.

The following are the most note-worthy and prominent dividend screeners.

The DARS Rating

The dividend advantage rating system is a tool that evaluates up to 2,000 stocks. The Dividend Advantage Rating System analyzes the dividends based on five metrics. Any rating above 3.0 thresholds can reduce the time and effort to select dividends options with better pay outs. A typical DARS would appear as below:

Rank Change	Stock Symbol	Company Name	DAR S™ Rating	Dividend Yield	Current Price	Ex-Div Date	ETF Alternative
1	99	ABC	3.5	20%	5.39%	$37.12	2020-01-09
3	97	XYZ	3.2	13%	6.70%	$47.11	2019-12-24
4	96	LDM	3.0	11%	2.52%	$149.58	2020-02-24

Market Cap and Sector

These are the two crucial factors to consider for picking up a successful investment plan. For instance, a company having diversified business line and increased market cap means that it can sustain its standing during tough situations. The company has the ability to increase its cash flows at any stage of its business cycle. Investing in such companies provides a higher margin for the investors with respect to future payouts.

As an investor, you must conduct a thorough research and consider companies that have at least 10 to 25 years of dividend increasing record. Certain companies including Target, Coca-Cola and Chevron Corp. have been increasing their dividend payouts regularly since the past six decades.

Strong Growth and Earnings

Another factor is to consider the companies with strong earnings and to compare that information with its technical indicators. Certain tools enable investors to rank the highest performing companies in terms of dividend payouts and provide them with the most watched stocks list. However, this feature is mostly available for premium users and provides a weekly update if certain preferred stocks are fluctuating. It also offers a live email option so investors can make faster decisions.

Dividend Stocks with Significant Track Records

Company	Sector	Consecutive annual dividend increase	Dividend yield
3M	Consumer industrials	60	2.7 %
Abbott Laboratories (ABT)	Healthcare	46	1.8 percent
AbbVie	Healthcare	46	5.4 percent
Aflac	Financial services	36	2.2 percent
Air Products & Chemicals	Basic materials	36	2.8 percent
A.O. Smith Corp.	Industrials	26	1.8 percent
Archer-Daniels Midland	Consumer defensive	43	3.2 percent
AT&T	Communications services	34	6.9 percent
Automatic Data Processing	Technology	44	2.2 percent
Becton Dickinson	Healthcare	47	1.3 percent
Brown-Forman Corp. (BF.B)	Consumer defensive	34	1.3 percent
Chevron Corp.	Energy	33	3.8 percent
Chubb	Financial services	26	2.2 percent
Cincinnati Financial Corp. (CINF)	Financial services	58	2.5 percent
Cintas Corp. (CTAS)	Industrials	36	1.1 percent
The Clorox Co.	Consumer defensive	41	2.5 percent

The Coca-Cola Co.	Consumer defensive	56	3.2 percent
Colgate-Palmolive Co.	Consumer defensive	55	2.6 percent
Consolidated Edison (ED)	Utilities	44	3.8 percent
Dover Corp. (DOV)	Industrials	63	2.2 percent
Ecolab	Basic materials	33	1.2 percent
Emerson Electric Co.	Industrials	62	3 percent
Exxon Mobil Corp.	Energy	36	4.4 percent
Federal Realty Investment Trust (FRT)	Real Estate	51	3 percent
Franklin Resources (BEN)	Financial services	37	3.4 percent
General Dynamics Corp. (GD)	Industrials	28	2.1 percent
Genuine Parts Co. (GPC)	Consumer cyclical	62	2.8 percent
Hormel Foods Corp. (HRL)	Consumer defensive	52	2 percent
Illinois Tool Works	Industrials	55	3 percent
Johnson and Johnson	Healthcare	56	2.7 percent
Kimberly-Clark Corp.	Consumer defensive	46	3.5 percent
Leggett & Platt	Consumer cyclical	47	3.5 percent
Lowe's Companies	Consumer cyclical	56	2 percent
McCormick & Co.	Consumer defensive	32	1.8 percent
McDonald's Corp.	Consumer cyclical	42	2.7 percent
Medtronic	Healthcare	41	2.3 percent
Nucor Corp.	Basic materials	45	2.7 percent
Pentair	Industrials	42	1.7 percent
Pentair United Financial	Financial services	25	4.1 percent
PepsiCo	Consumer defensive	46	3.3 percent
PPG Industries	Basic materials	46	1.8 percent

Procter & Gamble Co.	Consumer defensive	62	3 percent
Roper Technologies	Industrials	26	0.6 percent
S&P Global	Financial services	46	1 percent
Sherwin-Williams Co.	Basic materials	40	0.8 percent
Stanley Black & Decker	Industrials	51	2.1 percent
Sysco Corp.	Consumer defensive	48	2.4 percent
T. Rowe Price Group	Financial services	32	3 percent
Target Corp.	Consumer defensive	51	3.6 percent
United Technologies	Industrials	25	2.4 percent
V.F. Corp.	Consumer cyclical	46	2.4 percent
Walgreens Boots Alliance	Consumer defensive	43	2.5 percent
Walmart	Consumer defensive	44	2.2 percent
W.W. Grainger	Industrials	47	1.8 percent

Source U.S. News & World Report [7]

Sample Dividend Screener

A typical dividend screening tool would appear as below. If you notice, there are various factors to choose from while searching for preferred stocks and companies. As an investor, you may search by bargain stocks or tech giants. You may also seek information by the options of 52-week lows and highs. On the left-hand side, various filters are provided which allow investors to further compress the list by selecting choice of price, location

---

[7] https://money.usnews.com/investing/stock-market-news/slideshows/dividend-stocks-aristocrats?slide=55

and sector. Such screeners are eminent in maintaining a stellar portfolio as it saves a lot of time and effort from consulting a manual and independent research online. Moreover, these screeners are updated on a regular basis as they are internet integrated.

Source: MSN Money [8]

Selecting the Best Screener

Various screening tools are available with respect to the location of the investor or for the regions an investor is interested in. Stock Rover is the most favored screener for investors residing in America or Canada. For the investors residing out of these countries have the choice of using Metastock or Tradingview.

Metastock can be handy in terms of receiving technical analysis and also shows real-time news to the users. Tradingview encompasses almost all the stocks available

---

[8] https://www.msn.com/en-us/money/stockscreener/hdys

around the world and is the best choice for international investors.

Selecting the Dividend Investment Strategy

Before you decide to invest in certain stocks, make sure that you have a consistent and relevant strategy at hand. Primarily there are four main options to select from.

You may adopt the **safe dividend strategy** if you want to minimize the risk associated with stock investment. Make sure that the company is listed on well-regulated stock exchanges such as NASDAQ or NYSE. Also, consider the sales growth of the stocks higher than the dividend growth because it will be comparatively a more stable investment in the long run. It is important to make sure that the company has been paying a dividend for a long period of time and are highly capitalized.

A **high dividend yield strategy** stock is what a new investor will be looking at. But do note that a higher yield may also result in a significant drop in the price of the stock as well. While considering such companies, always make sure that the payout ratio does not exceed 60.

An aristocrat index or list of companies is important if you are investing in the **long-term** dividend growth strategy. Consider a screener that has a huge volume of historical data so that, as an investor, you have a pretty fair idea about the companies and their performance over the years.

You may also look into the ***dividend strategy + value*** criteria for screening. This strategy has been successfully used by well-known investors such as Ben Graham and Warren Buffet. The companies to look for under these criteria are the ones having low price to book, sales and earnings. Stock Rover can be of great help in this regard and can filter companies as per the lowest PE ratio within the same sector as well.

Invest in the Stocks

Once you are clear on the strategy you wish to adopt and screener to be used, the next step is to conduct research and begin buying the stocks. The user interface of this step may resemble as below:

In this step, you can also develop and maintain a watchlist according to your needs and requirements. The screener will inform you once there is any change in the stocks you are interested in. Also, this step will enable you to view the value score, dividend yield, fair value, and other relevant details.

Conduct a Thorough Research

Once you have the preferred companies on your list, make sure to check financial performance and historical growth patterns for the companies before you make a decision to buy stocks. Some screeners provide reports as well by conducting an intelligent financial analysis. This is known as the stock-rating system. It provides analysis based on:

- Dividend analysis

- Efficiency

- Growth

- Financial strength

- Growth

- Stock price momentum

Buy the Stocks

By the time you have come so far, it is safe to assume that as an investor, you have conducted complete research and are ready to invest. If your broker is charging you significantly, prefer using a non-commission-based broker. You certainly do not want to shell out a sum of money when it is comparatively easier to perform the task yourself.

Features Provided by the Screeners

The different screeners provide a lot of features so that even new investors have the ease of operating the process on their own. Some features are free of cost, whereas the advanced ones are offered only to premium members. Below are some of the features the investors are commonly provided to create their own dividend investment portfolio.

Dividend Calendar

Use this calendar to plan your annual income. This will show you the dividend payout dates as well as when to own the stocks in order to receive its dividend payout.

Dividend Aristocrats

This feature will enable you to view the most well-established stocks to own. This list is developed with certain criteria in place, and the featured companies are the ones that have shown continuous progress and improvement regardless of the economic slowdown.

High Yield Stocks

This feature is particularly suitable for investors seeking the dividend payout investment strategy. The investors can find the details of international companies offering high yield stocks.

Best Stocks

This area focuses upon the companies that have successfully grown their profits and dividend payout over a period of years.

Boost your Dividends

This feature is available for the premium investors and notifies the investor as the level of dividend yield fluctuates.

Profit Growth

The investor can find more information about the company; he is interested in investing in and analyzing the growth and performance based on the cash flows and corporate earnings.

Dividend Alarm Notification

This feature is quite helpful for investors in signaling the opportunities to buy and sell stocks on the basis of dividend yield. The investor can receive notifications in a number of choices and can stay updated without logging on the system every day.

Stock Screener

This area provides a lot of filter options for investors to choose from. All the stock details, dividend payout ratios, and yield are organized in a clear and concise format.

Rankings

The investor can creatively create rankings upon the selected criteria of their choice. The selected stocks will then be analyzed according to the metrics and produce a list of relevant stocks by creating a list through a ranking process

Important Note!

Owning dividends can be a lucrative income stream in the long run. However, there are certain other rules to follow.

❖ While buying the stocks, do not just consider the dividend payout ratio but analyze the performance of the company in the long run.

❖ The fund fees are often ignored initially while the investor is busy checking out for the most rewarding stocks to invest in. This may turn out to be an expense ratio, and therefore the fee charged must be taken into account. For instance, if stocks with the dividend yield of 4%

with the fund fees charged at 2.5 % per year, the investor is not left with many rewards.

CHAPTER 8

SAFE PORTFOLIO WITHDRAWAL

A common mistake that an investor makes, especially while the market is booming, is that they keep spending lavishly without realizing that their assets are depleting. To meet the expenses, the investors often draw money from their portfolio while it keeps on growing. Although this seems to be a positive situation, it can have serious repercussions once the market witnesses an economic slowdown.

There are various rules and strategies to adapt to ensure a safe withdrawal. Surprisingly, various studies conducted have revealed that more than 70% of American investors are not familiar with the available options.

Most of the investors have the desire to use the dividend payout to lead a comfortable life after retirement as well as to leave a considerable amount of wealth for the next generation. Both purposes are attainable provided that the investor has sufficient know-how of the outcomes of withdrawal on the overall dividend portfolio. The following section will cover the important steps for annual dividend withdrawal.

First of all, the investor must consider developing an annual expense sheet with all the possible expenses he or she will incur within the year. Once this is done, any income derived from other resources such as social security or pension must be recorded as well, and the expenses must be subtracted. The remaining amount will be the expenses that the investor will be taking out of the portfolio. This amount will be known as the withdrawal rate and will be deducted as part of the portfolio value. The time horizon is an important factor to consider, which refers to the life expectancy of the investor or the dependents.

The 4% Rule

In 1994, William Bengen proposed the four percent safe withdrawal rule according to which it is assumed that the stock investments will be on the safer side if the annual withdrawal rate of 4% is maintained. This means that the investor will not be outliving his portfolio.

Reasons for Dividend Withdrawal

In order to keep the dividend portfolio safe, the investor should consider not increasing the withdrawal rate every year. When the market has a recession or goes through an economic slowdown, it is important to reduce the withdrawal rate to mitigate any financial losses. The rate can then be picked up once the market maintains its normal levels. If your life expectancy is less than 15%, it is advisable to keep the withdrawal rate lower than 4%.

Selling a Dividend Stock

There may be various situations where the investor would like to sell the dividend stocks. However, it is advisable not to do so, especially in the case of high dividend-yielding companies with a consistent track record of growth.

However, there may be specific scenarios or needs of an investor that may require him to sell dividend stock. The following are a few insider tips to help you sell your dividend stock at the right time.

There are many reasons to sell the dividend stocks, including the following:

1- There may be times when a company may decide to reduce or eliminate the dividend payout. For instance, during the economic recession of 2008 and 2009, most of the companies could not retain favorable earnings and therefore had to cut down on the dividend payouts. The investor must keep an eye on the regularly published stock reports that show the cash flow of the companies as well as future projections. It is obvious that the risks must be mitigated in the initial stages, and therefore it is expected that the investor conduct authority searches and consider companies that have rarely reduced or eliminated dividend payouts in the past.

2- At times, when the stocks are overvalued, it is suggested to sell them and protect the savings. But here the investor is suggested to keep an eye on the industrial sector rather than just the company they have invested in because in case the former is overvalued, all the companies under the umbrella will be affected in terms of stock valuation. Also, it has been witnessed that high stock valuation is followed by a low dividend payout period. The investor must be cautious about this in order to keep the market in his favor at all times.

3- Investors must keep an eye on the weight of the stock position. There may be times when a few of the stocks may become a burden on your portfolio.

4- During the time when the stocks of a particular company begin to show high volatility levels, it is better to sell those stocks.

5- If the investor feels that he has lost confidence in a certain company, it is better to sell the stock. Even well-established companies show a disappointing trend depending upon the direction they are headed in. For instance, .an investors may enthusiastically invest in buying stocks of Microsoft or Target. However, in the future, the investor deems that one of the companies is headed in the wrong direction and therefore presents a risk for the dividend payout in the future. This is an indication for the investor to sell the stock.

6- Last but not least, an investor may have personal reasons to sell the stocks. Some unpredictable situations may add up to the decision or in case the investor decides to invest the money in another scheme for personal needs. Whatever the reason may be, the pros and cons must be weighed up with the utmost care in order to minimize the risk of financial loss to the investor.

CHAPTER 9

UNDERSTANDING THE DIVIDEND CALENDAR

The dividend calendar is the tool or option that informs or reminds the investor about the dividend payout dates. This can be a useful feature for investors so they can have an idea about their income schedule. Although companies pay out dividends on a quarterly basis, there are a few that consider twice a year. Below is a sample table to understand the concept of dividend payout dates.

AFH Financial	Jan 30, 2020	8	Feb 14, 2020	2.08%
Ag Growth Int (AFN)	Jan 30, 2020	2.4	Feb 14, 2020	5.06%
Ag Growth Int (AGGZF)	Jan 30, 2020	1.812	Feb 14, 2020	5.04%
AGNC Invest (AGNC)	Jan 30, 2020	0.48	Feb 11, 2020	10.43%
Alaris Royalty (AD)	Jan 30, 2020	1.65	Feb 18, 2020	7.36%
Alliant Energy (LNT)	Jan 30, 2020	0.38	Feb 18, 2020	2.57%
Allied Properties (AP_u)	Jan 30, 2020	1.65	Feb 18, 2020	2.98%
Ally Financial Inc (ALLY)	Jan 30, 2020	0.19	Feb 14, 2020	2.39%

American Core Sectors Dividend (ACZ)	Jan 30, 2020	0.55	Feb 14, 2020	4.08%
AFH Financial	Jan 30, 2020	8	Feb 14, 2020	2.08%
Ag Growth Int (AFN)	Jan 30, 2020	2.4	Feb 14, 2020	5.06%
American Hotel Income Properties LP (HOT_u)	Jan 30, 2020	0.8451	Feb 14, 2020	11.72%
Ames (ATLO)	Jan 30, 2020	0.24	Feb 14, 2020	3.53%
Antero Midstream (AM)	Jan 30, 2020	0.3075	Feb 12, 2020	20.30%
AO Smith (AOS)	Jan 30, 2020	0.24	Feb 18, 2020	2.11%
APQ Global (APQ)	Jan 30, 2020	6	Mar 02, 2020	8.76%
ARC Document Solutions (ARC)	Jan 30, 2020	0.01	Feb 28, 2020	3.08%
ARC Resources (ARX)	Jan 30, 2020	0.6	Feb 14, 2020	8.40%
Artis REIT (AX_u)	Jan 30, 2020	0.54	Feb 14, 2020	4.48%
Atrium Mortgage Investment Corp (AI)	Jan 30, 2020	0.9	Feb 12, 2020	6.14%
Australian REIT (HRR_u)	Jan 30, 2020	0.66	Feb 07, 2020	5.12%
Automotive Finco (AFCC)	Jan 30, 2020	0.2052	Feb 28, 2020	12.00%
Automotive Properties RE (APR_u)	Jan 30, 2020	0.804	Feb 14, 2020	6.40%
Badger Daylighting (BAD)	Jan 30, 2020	0.57	Feb 14, 2020	1.63%

CHAPTER 10

SIX COMMANDMENTS OF DIVIDEND INVESTING

Even though dividend investment is a potentially great source of generating income, it isn't a surefire way of earning profits. It comes bearing a lot of risks that an investor cannot always foresee. However, there are some cautious steps an investor can take to minimize losses. These steps are the ten rules, also called the "Ten Commandments of Dividend Investing." Any dividend investor that lives by these rules can hardly go wrong with his investments.

Most investors turn to dividend investment to earn a high yield. Many fraudulent companies, in current times, are more focused on personal gain rather than investor's interests. One can expect for promising dividend returns that hardly ever payout. It is also common for them to experience some turbulence where dividend payouts are concerned. Not only this, but the investors will slowly see a decline in the value of these stocks. This is why the first commandment is to avoid seeking higher yields. A smart investor will be prepared with relevant questions when higher yields are promised. The investor will inquire about and evaluate any risks that these yields might be exposed to.

For instance, a historical analysis revealed that REITs have been stable in terms of dividend payouts. They are a lucrative dividend investment entity and seem to be the first choice for most investors. However, the payout that they make from their earnings, as per the law, is so significant (90 percent), that the REITs are resulting in inconsistent payouts. This is because the REITs are accumulating debt due to the high percentage of payout. In addition to this, a higher yield may also lead to a decrease in the value of the stocks. This means that the investor might face a potential loss in the long run.

Thou Shalt Always Reinvest in Dividends

As much as one can stress the power of reinvesting dividends, it is hard to articulate just by using words. By reinvesting your dividends and using the compounding technique, you can exponentially grow your investments. Investors can also make use of the dividend reinvestment programs that often automatically allow you to reinvest the dividends without paying a commission. With time and as payouts increase, the payouts of the dividends continue to increase as well, leading to a compounding effect that will snowball over time. However, it should be mentioned that the dividend reinvestment option does not apply to those who are dependent on dividend income, such as retirees.

Honor Thy Tax Implications

Over the years, the process and tax structure of taxing dividends have seen major overhauls, additions, and modifications of policies and regulations so that a complete and equitable tax structure could be developed and implemented. Taxes on capital gains will more often or not fall below the taxes on standard income. If you happen to follow Warren Buffet, you are likely aware of his statement that he is taxed less than his secretary. Most of his income comes from dividends, which puts those gains in a lower tax bracket compared to salary or other types of compensation, and therefore, he is taxed at a lower rate.

Honor Thy Payout Ratio

When it comes to dividends and investing in them, the payout ratio stands as the most important factor as it highlights the company's ability to return the profits or pay the shareholders the returns they have been expecting. If the ratio comes out to be more than 100%, it means that a firm is paying more than it is earning, which is basically a red flag in the long run. Even though there is no such thing as a "sweet spot" when it comes to paying the dividends, anything nearing the 100% mark is always going to be a cause for concern.

You can take Verizon Wireless, for example. Its most fiscal year showed that it had earnings of $2.24, while it was expected that the forward year was to fall to $2.79. This is another example of estimating dividends, which leads to falsely high figures. This technique uses forward year EPS along with the current payout, a number of resources will use earnings of the most recent year and combine them with the dividend payout of the current year.

The investment opportunities in the U.S market are considered to be some of the highest. It is estimated that the US market constitutes 50 percent of the global investment. Even though the US market is strong and has many opportunities, an investor should not limit himself to this market alone. An investor should consider having multiple dividend investments, foreign as well as within the US market. What this strategy does is lower the risks of loss; if one market collapses, there is always a backup dividend income in place from other regions. For instance, the growing US and China trade war may result in fluctuation. While these two countries may take a hit, it could result in increased benefits for other foreign markets. As an investor who invests in local and foreign dividend investments, he won't suffer as big a loss as someone who solely invests in the US dividend investments.

If you decide on investing in foreign dividend investments, make sure you familiarize yourself with their local taxation policies to avoid any complications. In the US, tax policies are quite clear, and most investors are aware of them. One of the drawbacks of investing in foreign markets is that you won't find much information on it from people around you. Therefore, it is recommended to research as much as you can on their policies. For example, companies in the US are required by law to reveal their financial information to investors. However, this may or may not be the case for companies operating in other countries. Similarly, dividend payout policies may also differ. This is why it is strongly recommended that all investors find out all the information before taking the leap.

Once you've made sure you have all the information needed to invest in a foreign dividend investment, you might find it to be beneficial in many ways. For one, the cash payout is received by the investor in varying foreign currencies. This can be an advantage, especially if it is received from a country that has a stable and increasing currency value.

How many times have you fallen victim to the shelf that is marked with a 75% discount? It isn't easy to ignore your favorite - but expensive - truffle chocolates with more than half off. However, you bring the truffles home only to realize that they're so close to expiration, they'll go bad before you can even finish the pack. In reality, this purchase was, in fact, a loss, rather than a saving. Similarly, a company may show you high yielding investment opportunities, but not all that glitters is gold. The company might be tricking you into buying stocks with the promise of high yields when, in reality, it might be facing a considerable amount of loss.

To make sure you don't have to take a company's word for it, spend a considerable amount of time researching different companies and markets. A little time spent researching might help you avoid potentially high losses. And because large chunks of an investor's savings are invested in these companies, proper steps should be taken to avoid any hidden risks involved in dividend investments.

When an investor considers buying stocks, he should do deep research into the company's performance and dividend payouts. This is where many investors stumble. They run a background check on the company's performance in recent years. However, it makes more sense to check the record of the company for at least the past decade. A company that has a consistent increase in dividend payouts is considered to be stable for investment. Moreover, the investor must also conduct thorough research to ensure that the company has complete transparency and isn't tricking investors by showing good financial performance. The growth of dividend payouts is only good in the case that the company does not have a high debt ratio, and is consistently growing in terms of its operations and product demand.

On the other hand, companies who are constantly raising their dividend payouts are under pressure as well. This can lead the management toward making riskier investments, and therefore, it is important for the investors to pay close attention and stay put with the financials of the company.

Thou Shalt be Wary of Value Traps

Value trap, a phenomenon where a dividend may yield strong returns, and the stock might look cheap because the price might have been dropping, make the stock look like a false buy. The first sign of a value trap is a company paying excessive dividend payouts when the cash flow has been falling as compared to its competitors. Value traps happen to draw in the savviest of investors. Therefore, it is important for them to be careful while investing in stocks.

Though Shalt be Mindful of Special Dividends

A company may sometimes initiate special dividends such as a special one-time dividend payout. Microsoft, for example, issued a large dividend back in 2004. Investors should keep an eye out for such stocks as things may seem rosier than normal. There is, of course, a huge difference between a one-time payout and standard dividend payouts. One thing investors should do in such cases is to look at statistics, particularly the history of payouts. While picking out the dividend stocks to invest in, investors should look into history to observe the payout patterns and behaviors of each company.

Though Shalt Not Make Dividends Thy Only Priority

As it has been assessed that dividends are a great way to invest in a consistent stream of income. However, it should not be the only metric to abide by. Every security has a certain set of fundamentals that make it right or wrong, and many times it will not have to do anything with the payout of the dividends. Therefore, it is imperative for investors to ensure and understand how a company operates and its future position. A strong company is better than a weak company that has strong yields.

Dividend's Worst Year

The economic recession of 2008 was significantly high after the Great Depression and the stock market lost more than half of its value. The financial shock made most of the well-established companies make decisions differently from the standard and traditional rules as they succumbed to financial losses. The real estate investors and the companies faced a serious cash crunch, and because of this, the dividend payout by the companies was significantly decreased. Standard and Poor reported that more than 800 stocks out of 7,000 had to cut the payouts. Companies including General Electric, Dow Chemical, and Pfizer were hard hit over a period of many decades, and it is estimated that the investors faced the financial loss of over $58 billion.

The S&P 500 report reveals that out of the dividend-paying companies, 78 drastically cut their dividend payout to approximately 21%. However, on the other hand, a few companies did increase the dividend payouts. The 363 stocks that performed well made up 73% of the index and provided a pool of opportunities for investors. This also refers to the fact that the companies listed in the S&P 500 indexes are mostly profit-making. However, the stability issue is still not guaranteed.

Situations like these have a lot of lessons to teach dividend investors. It is important to understand that investing in stocks can be a risky business, especially if the cautionary measures are ignored.

A few well-known strategies for picking up stocks can be beneficial. These approaches can be merged in order to get better yields. There are no hard and fast rules that can guarantee a persistent income generation, but by implementing a few strategies, risks associated with dividend investment growth can be mitigated.

CHAPTER 11

CASE STUDIES- BUILDING A SUCCESSFUL PORTFOLIO

Building a successful portfolio requires patience, research, and observation of how companies behave. It is not only about buying dividends and then waiting for the yields. Instead, it is also about diversifying your portfolio so you can create additional income streams. Take Bill Gates and Warren Buffet, for example. They are still the kings of investment, and with time, have developed a habit of investing in stocks that carry the least amount of risk. Let us discuss them a bit.

Bill Gates

Berkshire Hathaway, Inc.

Berkshire Hathaway happens to be the largest holding firm in Bill Gate's dividend foundation portfolio. The foundation owns 54 million shares of Berkshire

Hathaway with a value of just under $10 Billion. Berkshire Hathaway is one of the biggest companies in the S&P 500, with a market capitalization of $51184 billion and in 2017 was ranked second on fortune 500.

Microsoft

The second-largest holding company in the foundation is Bill Gate's own, Microsoft. The foundation owns 32 million shares of the company at a value of nearly $3.12 billion. Microsoft is one of the biggest companies in the S&P 500, with a market capitalization of $825 billion and was ranked 28th on Fortune 500 in 2017.

Caterpillar

Caterpillar is the third-largest company in the foundation's portfolio. The foundation happens to own over 11 million shares of Caterpillar at a market value of over $1.5 billion. Caterpillar is a member of Dow stock and specializes in making heavy machinery and equipment used for mining, energy, and agriculture. It possesses a market capitalization of $86.48 billion. Caterpillar was ranked 65th in 2017 on Fortune 500.

Waste Management

The fourth-largest company in the foundation's portfolio is Waste Management, Inc. The foundations hold more than 18.6 million shares at a market rate of $1.52 billion. Waste management is responsible for providing waste management and other environment associated services. It happens to be the largest waste management business in the country, with over 21 million customers. The company has a market capitalization of $39.55 billion and was ranked 202 in 2017 on Fortune 500.

Canadian National Railway Company

The fifth-largest company in the portfolio of the foundation is the Canadian National Railway Company. The foundation owns 17.1 million shares of the company at a market value of $1.4 billion. Canadian National Railway Company provides services related to integrated transportation such as freight forwarding, trucking, and warehousing. The company is mainly responsible for transporting petroleum products, fertilizers, coals, metals, and automotive products. The company has a market capitalization of $65 billion.

The purpose of mentioning the companies above was to observe and notice the fact that Bill Gates is interested in companies that have large market capitalization and have a strong grip in the markets where they operate. This provides Bill Gates an idea of how risky or fruitful investing in a company would be.

Warren Buffett

Warren Buffet, who is also known as "the Oracle of Omaha," believes in diversifying his portfolio. Even though he has comparatively fewer shares in the communication and consumer discretionary sector that does not draw him toward selling the stocks. As long as the company is moving towards growth, it will have Warren Buffet's attention.

He has famously said that even if he had a small investment, he could compound it to 50% in about a year's time. That is confidence and belief in his skills and knowledge of the industry. As a new investor, the best decision you can make is to follow the footsteps of those who have tread on the path before. And Warren Buffet's investment strategies are one for the folklores.

Buffet has pretty basic principles that he follows. And that perhaps is one of his strongest qualities - that no matter how the market is doing, he will follow his principles to yield higher returns in the long run. He believes people should only invest in companies that showcase 'sold fundamentals and potential for continuous growth.'

At the core of it, the concept is pretty basic, but what is difficult is its implementation in the real world. But if he can take $10,000 and turn it into a net worth over $86 billion, then there is little doubt that his strategies work. He has also managed to create a value of over $400 billion for his shareholders. Here is a look at his portfolio.

46.04% of his Portfolios consist of Financials

These include insurance companies and money center banks. He owns stakes in multiple companies, including Wells Fargo, Bank of America, JPMorgan Chase, US Bancorp, Moody's, Bank of NY Mellon, Goldman Sachs, Visa, Travelers, MasterCard, Synchrony Financial and Globe Life among others.

Over 25% of His Portfolio is invested in the Information Technology Sector

Maybe calling it the entire sector is a stretch. Buffet solely invests in Apple when it comes to technology. But he invests heavily! For every $4, more than $1 is invested or tied up with the technology giant.

15% of His investments are Tied Up in Consumer Staples

These have seen a dip in recent years. Berkshire Hathaway's investment in this sector has dipped down from over 45% to around a decade ago, to just 15% in current times. Currently, he owns shares in Kraft Heinz, Coca-Cola, Procter & Gamble, Costco, and Mondalez International. Coca-Cola takes up 10% of this consumer portfolio, where the remaining 5% is divided among other companies.

4.71% is invested in Transports

Going by his mantra to truly diversify one's portfolio, less than 5% is invested in transport, mainly airlines.

Buffet entered this sector during the middle of the last decade, in 2016, and there are speculations that his investments in this sector will likely increase in the near future. These investments include Delta Airlines, American Airlines Group, Unite Airlines Group, and UPS.

His decision to invest in airlines in specific has met with a lot of confusion and debate because amongst all his other investments; this one seems to be a bit on the riskier side. Airlines have a track record of not being able to survive economic downturns, but again, one can muse over his investment decisions, but one knows better than to question them. One reasoning could be the plunging prices of crude oil, which have made airlines quite profitable in recent years.

And Others

The remaining less than 10% has been invested in a variety of sectors, including communications, real estate, materials, healthcare, consumer discretionary, and energy. The companies include VeriSign, Charter Communications, Phillips 66, Occidental Petroleum, and Johnson & Johnson, among many others.

The dividend investment growth portfolio of Warren Buffet.

Ticker	Name	Sector	Industry	Dividend Yield	Dividend Safety
AAL	American Airlines Group	Industrials	Airlines	1.49	33
AXP	American Express Company	Financials	Consumer Finance	1.3	80
AAPL	Apple	Information Technology	Technology Hardware, Storage and Peripherals	0.97	99
BAC	Bank of America Corporation	Financials	Diversified Banks	2.17	89
BK	Bank of New York Mellon Corporation	Financials	Asset Management and Custody Banks	2.76	73
KO	Coca-Cola Company	Consumer Staples	Soft Drinks	2.81	80
COST	Costco Wholesale Corporation	Consumer Staples	Hypermarkets and Super Centers	0.84	99
DAL	Delta Air Lines	Industrials	Airlines	2.8	61
GM	General Motors Company	Consumer Discretionary	Automobile Manufacturers	4.52	61
GL	Globe Life	Financials	Life and Health Insurance	0.66	92
GS	Goldman Sachs Group	Financials	Investment Banking and Brokerage	2.06	91
JNJ	Johnson & Johnson	Healthcare	Pharmaceuticals	2.54	99
JPM	JPMorgan Chase & Co.	Financials	Diversified Banks	2.68	79
KHC	Kraft Heinz Company	Consumer Staples	Packaged Foods and Meats	5.31	29

MA	Mastercard Incorporated	Information Technology	Data Processing and Outsourced Services	0.5	99
MDLZ	Mondelez International	Consumer Staples	Packaged Foods and Meats	2.08	66
MCO	Moody's Corporation	Financials	Financial Exchanges and Data	0.77	83
MTB	M&T Bank Corporation	Financials	Regional Banks	2.58	99
OXY	Occidental Petroleum Corporation	Energy	Integrated Oil and Gas	7.67	50
PSX	Phillips 66	Energy	Oil and Gas Refining and Marketing	3.72	65
PNC	PNC Financial Services Group	Financials	Regional Banks	3.07	82
PG	Procter & Gamble Company	Consumer Staples	Household Products	2.37	99
QSR	Restaurant Brands International	Consumer Discretionary	Restaurants	3.19	62
SIRI	Sirius XM Holdings	Communications	Cable and Satellite	0.75	61
LUV	Southwest Airlines Co.	Industrials	Airlines	1.25	99
STOR	STORE Capital Corporation	Real Estate	Diversified REITs	3.59	61
SU	Suncor Energy	Energy	Integrated Oil and Gas	4.02	71
SYF	Synchrony Financial	Financials	Consumer Finance	2.7	53

CONCLUSION

The challenging times and ever-changing business landscape are encouraging many people to seek out various income-generating options. Retirees are often faced with various options to choose from in order to invest their savings, maximize rewards while minimizing the risks associated with their investments. With various investment options available in the market, the dividend investment strategy seems to be a safer and more stable investment option

Dividend investments can help individuals prepare for retirement, create exponential wealth, and make smarter financial decisions for themselves and their families. However, all this requires in-depth research and more than just monetary investment. This book can only offer guidance, but its implementation is up to you.

It is quite easy to gain information and study successful investors, but the application is the difficult part. While knowledge about the subject can influence decision making, it can be difficult to make the right decisions in the heat of the moment when your money is on the line.

A good idea would be to create a system and stick to the system, no matter how simple or complex it seems. Does it mean you should be carrying weights of dead horses or dead investments? Of course not! It just means don't make impulsive decisions but rather wait for markets to stabilize and offer the returns it promised!

You also need to keep your goals at the forefront. Your investments require a path, a destination in order to organically grow in the right direction. I hope this book has helped you find your path to tread on with your investments. All the best and good luck!

SWING TRADING

A Strategic Guide to Swing Trading in Stocks, Options, and Futures for Beginners

Joey Thompson

INTRODUCTION

In the following chapters I will discuss everything that you need to know in order to get yourself started on swing trading and to make sure that you can bring in a lot of money in no time. There are a ton of great options that you can use when you want to invest your money, and there are even a number of other options that work on the stock market as well. but nothing will provide you with the same return on investment, and the same ease of use, as we can find when we work on swing trading.

This guidebook will take some time to talk about swing trading and all the steps that you need to follow to get started on this in no time. This is a great strategy to use that allows you to have a bit more time to wait for the big changes in a stock price, while still earning a good profit in a shorter amount of time compared to some of your other strategies.

To start our adventure, we are going to take a look at swing trading and some of the basics that it entails. We will look more at what swing trading is and then dive into some of the benefits of using this trading method over some of the others. We will even take a look at how this kind of investment strategy is different than day trading, though the two do have a lot of things in common.

When we are done with that, it is time to move on to some of the steps that you need to take, and some of the things that you need to consider when you are ready to make your first official trade in swing trading. Don't worry, this is a whole lot easier to work on than it may seem, and you can enter the market in no time once you have those basic steps down.

From that point, it is time to get into a few of the strategies that we need to follow in order to see success with the swing trading strategy. For starters, we need to focus a bit on the idea of the technical and the fundamental analysis. We will discuss these a bit throughout the whole guidebook because they are so important and can make a world of difference in the results that you can get, but we will take a few chapters to explore each of these on their own. This can help us to see the benefits of each and can make it easier to determine which one we should use for our trading.

Then it is time to move on to some of the different things that we need to know in order to use swing trading on the different securities. We will focus mainly on how to trade in stocks with this strategy, but it is possible to also work with options like futures, commodities, the Forex market, and more and still see some great results. We will take some time to discuss this through this guidebook.

Then we can end this guidebook with a discussion on some of the best options when you want to pick out a strategy. These strategies can help us out with knowing when to enter the market and when to exit, and they are used by beginners and professionals in this market all of the time. We will look at some of the most common strategies, so you are set to get the best out of this process in no time.

This may seem like a lot of information when we first get started with the swing trading market. But this is also a really profitable way for us to learn how to invest and make money on the market as some trends like to change. It is one of the most efficient methods of trading, and it comes with the lowest amount of risk as well. when you are ready to learn more about swing trading and how you can use it to make money as well, make sure to check out this guidebook to get started.

There are plenty of books on this subject on the market, thanks again for choosing this one! Every effort was made to ensure it is full of as much useful information as possible, please enjoy!

CHAPTER 1

HOW TO GET STARTED IN SWING TRADING

Investing is a great way to take your money and make it grow. And if you get down the right strategy and learn how to make this work for you, you will be able to get some really great return on investment without having to work on it full time. There are actually quite a few options when it is time to invest, and you are sure to find the one that works the best for you in no time. But one of the best options that will help you to earn a lot of money in a short amount of time, but is not as risky or as stressful as day trading, includes a method known as swing trading.

What Is Swing Trading

We first need to take a look at swing trading and what this is all about. To start, swing trading is a style of trading that we can use to capture the gains that happen in a stock or any other financial security that we want to use, over a period of a few days to several weeks. These traders are going to work with technical analysis to help them find the right opportunities for trading and to help them make some more money. There are timeswhen the fundamental analysis is a better choice for the swing trader because it allows them a new way to look at the patterns and the trends in prices.

Both of this analysis is going to be important. But they do work in completely different ways, so we have to understand when to use each one. The good news is that we will talk about both of these and how each one works later on in this guidebook so you can get the best results with this in no time.

This is just the start of what we need to know to start with swing trading; there is so much more that we can focus on as well. for the most part, the process of swing trading will involve holding onto a position, doing so either long or short, for more than one trading session. This is the difference between swing trading and day trading. The day trader will purchase security and has to sell it by the end of the day. The swing trader is still on a short term strategy, but they can have anywhere from two days to two weeks to decide to hold onto the stock or to sell it for a profit or a loss.

The swing trader gets a little bit more time to work with the stocks than a day trader, but they usually need to get rid of the stocks, either for a profit or a loss, within a few weeks. There are some trades that last for a few months and can follow this option, but it is important that you only hold onto the stocks for a short amount of time before doing this strategy. Holding onto them for months or years turns you out of swing trading and over to some of the other options. Those are great ways to invest as well, and if you want to mix it up sometimes, holding onto stocks for longer can work well too, but this is not swing trading.

In a few cases, a swing trade can start out with us planning to use it for a few days, and then we get out of the trade during the same trading session. This is a rare option, and usually, the swing trader will only use it when the conditions are really volatile, and it is hard to know where they will go after this

The goal of working with swing trading is that we want to go through and capture a chunk of a price move we think will happen in the future. While there are some traders who like to look for stocks with a lot of volatility in them, some others like to work with a stock that is more sedated. No matter which one you choose to go with, the process that comes with swing trading asks us to identify where the price of the asset is most likely to move next, entering into a position based on that information and then getting some of the profits from that move if it does show up.

Most successful swing traders are only looking to capture a bit of the potential price movement. Then they are ready to get out of the trade before things reverse, and then move on to the next opportunity that comes out there. As you learn how to read charts better and understand more about the stock market or the security market that you want to work with, you will get better at handling some of the ups and downs of the market, and you can make some good decisions on how to do your trades.

There are a few things that we can consider when it comes to working with swing trading, and that we need to review before we go through with some more information on swing trading and what we can do with it. These points will include:

1. This kind of trading will involve the trader taking some trades that will last a few days up to a few months to help the trader make some profits from the price moves that they anticipate.

2. Swing trading is a good way to trade, but the trader has to be ready to see that there are risks for staying in the market over the weekend and overnight if they choose this strategy. It is possible that the price cold gap and open at a

really different price by the next day or after the weekend.

3. Swing traders are able to take some profits with the help of the risk to reward ratio based on the profit target and the stop loss, or they are able to take some losses or profits based on some of the price action movements or the technical indicators along the way.

Swing trading is often seen as one of the most popular forms of trading because there is a lot of potential profit that can be made out of it. This option allows the trader to look for some opportunities that will show up within a few weeks, and then they can capitalize on it. This can make some good money in the short term, without being as risky and volatile as getting in and out of the market quickly with day trading.

If you decide that swing trading is the right option for you, then you should have a really good familiarity and understanding of how technical analysis works. We will talk about some of the specifics that come with this option later, but basically, it involves looking at lots of different charts and figuring out the best course of action based on some of the trends that show up in the market. Adding a bit of knowledge about the news and how that can affect the stocks and whether that will keep things following the trends or disrupting them, can make a difference in how much success you can see with this kind of trading.

Many traders who use this strategy are going to assess the trades based on the risk to reward ratio that shows up with this one. When they are able to take the time to analyze the chart of one of the assets they are interested in, they can then determine where they will enter the market, where they would like to place the stop losses, and then they can anticipate the likely profit they will make if the trade goes their way.

We have to really think through some of these trades to get the best deal. If you are risking $1 a share on a setup that is likely going to give you $3 in profit, this is going to be favorable in terms of the risk and reward you are taking. If you are doing this and the reward is only $1 or even lower, then this is not a good option to work with. You need to be reasonable with this. What is the likelihood that you will get the profits that you want, without being unreasonable in the process?

Most swing traders like to work with technical analysis because there are some short-term natures that come with the trades. This is important to learn how to do, but sometimes a fundamental part added into it is a good idea as well because it enhances the analysis that you can get. For example, if a swing trader is taking a look at things and notices that there is a bullish setup in the stock, then they may ais want to verify that the fundamentals of the asset are looking favorable at the same time.

Swing traders will often take some time to look at the daily charts and see whether there are some good opportunities that they can jump on. It is common that they can look at the hour or the 15-minute charts to see whether there is something for them to jump on, and it can help them to find the right stop loss, take profit, and entry levels that will make them the most money possible.

There are a few benefits and negatives that we can see when we look at swing trading. We will take a look at some of the positives first:

1. This will require less of your time than day trading and can give you more profits with less work.

2. It helps us to maximize some of the short-term profit potentials because it is easier to catch some of the market swings that happen.

3. It is possible to work just with a technical analysis of this one and see some great profits out of it. When we only have to work with one type of analysis, it is a lot easier to trade and can make the process easier.

While there are a number of benefits to working with swing trading, we also need to focus on some of the reasons why people are warry about using this kind of trading strategy at all. Some of the negatives that come with swing trading include:

1. Some of the positions that you use will be subject to risks that occur overnight and on the weekends. This can make it a lot riskier to get the work done.

2. If the market does a big reversal on you, this can create big losses that are hard to work with.

3. Sometimes a swing trader will miss out on some of the longer-term trends because they are focusing just on the short-term market moves that they see

How Is Swing Trading Different From Day Trading

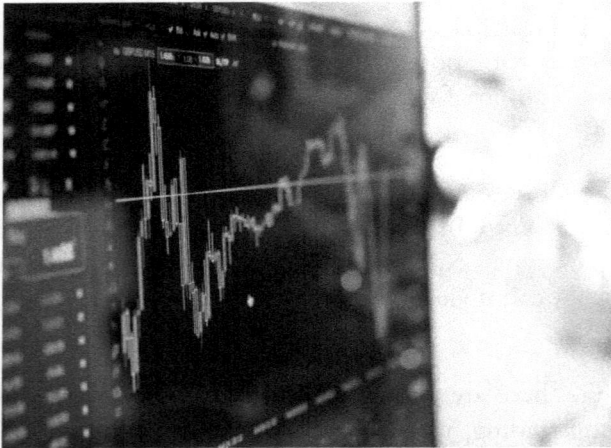

If you have spent some time learning about day trading in the past, you may feel like there are a lot of similarities that show up between the two trading strategies. There are a few differences that show up here, but there are also a few things that can make this kind of trading similar, and as a beginner, it is hard to know the similarities and the differences between these two styles of trading.

The main difference that shows up between the swing trading and the day trading is the amount of time you spend in the market and hold your position. With swing trading, you will hold onto the position at least overnight, and often for a few days and then you will close out the position. The day trader is going to close out their position before the market has a chance to close on the same day they purchase the security. So, to keep it simple, day traders will purchase and sell their positions in one day, and then the swing trader will hold onto the position for up to a few weeks.

Because they hold onto the position overnight, it is likely the swing trader will have to deal with some form of unpredictability from the overnight risk. This could be things like gaps and a down against the position. By taking on the overnight risk, these trades are made with some smaller position sizes compared to what we see with day trading, making the assumption that the two traders would have the same sized account. The day trader is more likely to work with position sizes that are larger because they can take that risk out.

A swing trader is going to also have some access to margin or leverage up to 50 percent. This means that if the trader has been approved to do something known as margin trading, they would only need to have $25,000 of their own capital to make the trade, but the margin would allow them to trade up to $50,000.

Tactics to Use With Swing Trading

There are a lot of great tactics that a swing trader is able to utilize to get the best results. We will look at a few of these in more detail at the end of this guidebook, but we can certainly look at a few of the basics now and see how this works. To start, it is common for a swing trader to look at multi-day chart patterns. Some of the common patterns that they will look at including the average crossovers, the head, and shoulders patterns, cup and handle patterns, triangles, and flags. The choice you make in a strategy is going to depend on how the market is working and what seems to make the best sense for your trades.

Each swing trader who gets into the market has to come up with their own plan and strategy that provides them an edge over other traders. This will involve looking for trade setups that can lead to movements that are predictable in the price of the asset. This is not an easy thing to work on, and there isn't a single setup or strategy out there that is going to behave and work each time that you use it.

The good news is that if you work with a good risk and reward ratio, then it isn't necessary to win each time in order to get ahead. The more favorable the risk to reward strategy, the fewer times that you need it to win in order to get the profit that you want overall in many of your trades.

The Benefits of Swing Trading

Before we end this chapter, we need to take a quick look at some of the benefits that you can get when you decide to use swing trading as your method of trading overall. There are a lot of options for investing, and they can all provide you with some benefits and some reasons as to why you should use this one over one of the other choices. But there are a ton of benefits as to why swing trading is the best one here, and why you should at least consider adding it to your toolbelt if you want to be successful here.

Some of the benefits that you can enjoy when it comes to swing trading include:

1. It is easy to work with: if you have never done any kind of investing before, you may be pleasantly surprised at how easy swing trading in the stock market can be. It doesn't take as much work as some of the other options, and as long as you can look over the stocks and the trends that come with the many charts you should be looking over, you will be able to start this up without a lot of problems either.

2. It doesn't require a lot of money to get started:
    Of course, the more money that you can safely
    invest in the market, the more that you can
    potentially earn. But even if you just have a
    little bit of money, you will find that this will
    work out well. this is a great starting point for
    those who have been trying to get into some
    kind of investment but don't have a ton of
    money to spare in the process.

3. It has less risk than other options. Compared
    to working with day trading and even some of
    the other types of investments out there, swing
    trading can carry much less risk. It provides us
    with a good amount of profit for a lot less risk,
    so that is positive for each investor who would
    like to give it a try.

4. It can work on any stock or security. You will
    also find that when you work a bit with swing
    trading, it is a fantastic way for us to make
    some good profits whether we work with the
    stock market or with some other type of
    security. We will speed most of this guidebook
    talking about how to use this in relation to the
    stock market, but a lot of the information can
    be changed to work with other securities as
    well. this gives you some freedom to try
    different things.

5. It can bring in quite a bit of profit: If you do
    this well, and you take the time to really learn
    about the stocks and what they have to offer
    along the way, there is a ton of potential to

make money on these kinds of trades. This is not a get rich quick kind of scheme, and you will have to stick with it and put in some work if you would like to turn this into a viable way to make some money or an income, but it is a lot easier than spending hours at work hoping to get a raise.

As we can see here, there are a lot of reasons why someone would want to consider working with swing trading and making this a big part of their process as well. When you can take a look at some of the charts and graphs that come with it, and you pay attention to the trends and what they are saying, you will find that this is one of the best ways to make money in the stock market.

CHAPTER 2

HOW TO PREPARE FOR YOUR FIRST TRADE

Now that we have had some time to learn more about swing trading and what it entails, it is time for us to move on and learn a bit more about how to actually enter into a trade like this and how we can do it well so that we make some profits. This process does have a few steps that we should spend our time on, but it is not difficult. Once you set up your own account and find a good broker who can walk you through all of this, you will find that the process is as simple as can be. Some of the steps that you can take when it is time to prepare for our very first trade as a swing trader includes:

Find a Good Broker

One of the important decisions that you will make when you first get started in trading is who you will hire as your broker. This is a really important decision and one that you need to take some time, and perform some research on, to make sure that you are prepared and will have the right one. There are many brokers out there, so this can be a hard decision.

The first thing to determine is how much time you plan to put into your investing, and how much help you will need. Some people like to do the work all on their own, and others will need some hand-holding to get them started at least. There are brokers out there that can help with both situations; you just need to know what your situation is before you start looking.

Then you need to take a look at some of the fees that the broker is going to charge. If the fees are too high, then they will start to eat into your profits, and that is never a good thing. All brokers are going to charge you some fees in order to invest and use them, so that is something you should expect right from the beginning. However, the way they charge these fees, and the amount that you spend on these fees over time is going to really depend on each individual broker.

Some will charge you for each transaction you do. This can work well for some of the long-term investments because you won't move your position all that much during that time. But as a swing trader, it is likely that you will make a lot of trades on a regular basis, so this may add up quickly. Others will charge you based on a percent of how much you make as you go through the process.

There isn't a right or wrong way that the brokers will charge their fees to you, but you do need to be careful and know how this is done before you jump in. talk to your broker about this ahead of time because you do not want to be surprised by the fees and some of the other parts that you weren't aware of after you enter the trades.

You can also take some time to look more at some of the features and special incentives that the broker is going to offer to you. These will change based on the broker you want to use, but they can be a great way to get you ahead and are offered just because the broker is trying to get some new clients through the door. This is beneficial for you, so you might as well use it at least a little bit.

And finally, it is often a good idea to go through and talk with your broker, at least a little bit. This will make it easier to get to know them and figure out if their style is similar to yours. If you don't feel comfortable with one broker over another, then this is a good sign that you should choose someone else. You could be with this broker for a long period of time if things work out, so you need to be comfortable with using them as well.

Decide How Much You Can Spend

This is a tricky one to work with because the amount will depend on your own personal budget. Any amount can be used to make trading profitable. But you do have to keep in mind to never trade more than you can afford to lose. Too many new traders will just throw some money into the market, assuming that they will get rich in a few weeks and get their money back in no time. And then they make the wrong decisions about trading and lose all of that money, money that they really had needed for something else.

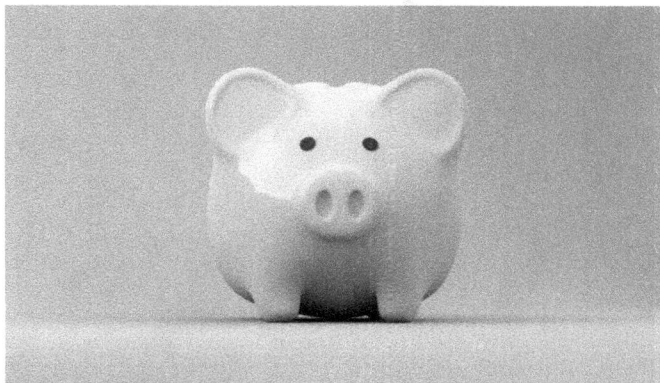

That is one of the number one rules that we have to follow when it comes to trading is to never use money that we can't afford to lose. This may seem silly and may keep us back from purchasing as many stocks as we would like, but it is one way to limit the amount of risk that we take on with swing trading. And swing trading, just like other forms of trading and investing, does carry some risk.

One way to make sure that you follow this rule is to set up a separate account that you would like to use just for trading money. Each month, add in the amount that you can safely invest, without hurting your other finances, and that is all that you can trade on. That way, if you make a few bad trades, you have not lost all of the money that you need for making the house payment or something else that needs to be paid that month.

Do Some Research

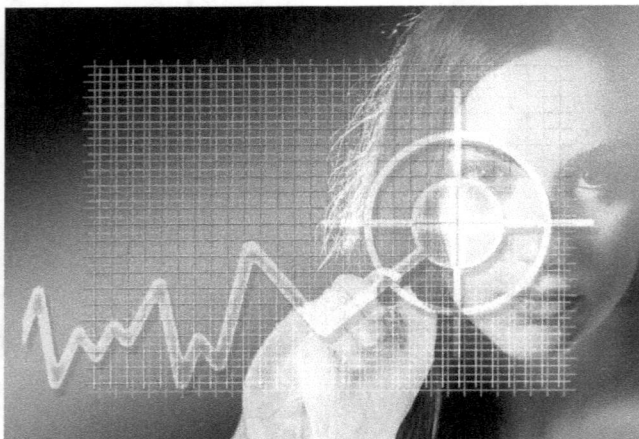

Research is your best friend when you go through this process. The more time that you can spend researching and look at charts, the more that you will understand how the market works and how much you can make on it in the process. No one has done well in the stock market, no matter what their strategy is, without first doing some research to help them out here.

There are a number of sources that you can use in order to get your research done and to make sure that you really like the results at the end in terms of profits. Charts and graphs about the stock market, and about the particular security that you want to spend time on will be your first source. Swing traders like to spend a lot of time working with technical analysis, so these charts and graphs are going to be so important in your work.

In addition to these charts, there are a few other resources that you can spend your time on to make sure that you see the best results and that you can really take your trading to the next level. News sources are a good place to start because they can provide you with some really great information that the company is releasing or what other analysts are saying as well. Then you can also look at some of the financial records of the company to see whether it is in good standing and is likely to play along with your plan for as long as you need it too.

There are a lot of benefits that come with working on swing trading, but you need to have a plan in place, and you need to make sure that you have done your research. There is a lot that can happen on the stock market in a short amount of time, so being prepared and making sure that you know what is going on with your chosen companies can help you to see more profits.

Find Some Good News Sources to Use

While the technical analysis is a good option to use, and lots of charts will become your best friends when going through this process, you should also consider looking through some news sources, ones that you trust, and can keep you up to date on a regular basis. You will become best friends with these, and they can guide a lot of the trades that you want to do.

Sometimes, the big swings that you see in the market the ones that will make swing trading more successful than other types of trades are the ones that are based on news that a company releases about itself. This news can make a difference in which stocks and securities that you would like to purchase, and if you know that these releases are about to come out, you can use this to your advantage to get ahead and make some good profit.

Let's say that you are reading the news and you see that Company A is about to do a big expansion in the area. They will add new jobs and some new products that you think will sell really great. You may see that this is all about to be released in the next few weeks. You may make the prediction that once the company releases all of this information and shares it with stockholders and others, it will make the value of the company go up and raise its stocks.

So, with that information in hand, you go to your broker and take a look. You notice that the stock price is doing well and has for some time, but you are predicting that it is going to rise really high in the next few weeks or so as others start to take a bigger interest in this company and what it has to offer. If the risk to reward ratio that you calculate out makes sense, then you purchase as many of that stock as you can and hold onto it.

If you were right, the company, sometime in the next few weeks, will release information to the public, and the public will go wild. Everyone will want to be a part of the changes that Company A is introducing, and they will purchase up the stock. Now the price of the stock starts to rise really quickly because the demand is a lot higher. When it finally gets to the point where you feel comfortable making a profit, you will sell off your shares and pocket the difference.

This is a really successful method to use when you want to work on swing trading. It will allow you a chance to go through and get into the market and make a purchase before the price goes up, and then you can sell when the price is high. You have to work with some really reputable news sources, and you have to be able to catch some of the smaller items that are in those news sources to make sure that you can make the most profit possible.

Consider the Good Risk to Reward for Your Trade

It is so important that you come up with a good risk to reward ratio for any trades that you complete. And this risk to reward ratio has to make sense. You will not be able to make $100,000 on a trade unless you have millions to invest in the stock. The stocks are not likely to go up that much in just a few weeks, so get that idea out of your head right now. However, you can make $100,000 a year on these trades, though you will have to do them over and over again during the year if you have the right risk to reward ratio.

As we mentioned a bit in the previous chapter, a good risk to reward ratio would be if you spent $1 on a stock, and you thought this trade could potentially bring you $3. The risk is higher than the potential loss that you could suffer, so it is a good one to use, especially if it looks pretty certain that the market will move in the direction that you want.

On the other side of things, if you put the money into the market and your reward was only $.50 for the $1 that you spent, it is likely that this is going to be too risky to work with. We want the reward to be as high as possible compared to the risk that we take. This helps us to make some good profits, with less risk, even if the stocks don't go up as high as we would like.

When you take a look at a few of the charts and other things that are important to this process, you need to make sure that you look closely at the risk to reward ratio that you will deal with. This can change based on which stocks you are following and what kind of trade you would like to do. But before you enter into the trade, you need to know pretty well whether this trade is going to be worth your time or not.

Completing the First Trade

Now that we have taken some time to go through the other steps, it is time to actually complete your first trade. Make sure that you already have the money you would like to spend on trading in your account. This usually takes a few days to process, so having it set up and ready to go inside of your account can help you to start trading right away. Do this while working on some of the research and deciding all the other parts.

By this time, you should already have a good idea of which stocks are going to be the ones that you would like to purchase. When the stocks reach a point that seems like a good discount, or at least will provide you with the reward ratio that you want if the trend goes in your direction, then it is time to make the purchase and get the number of stocks that you want.

Decide on the entry price that you want to use. How much are you willing to spend on each stock from the start? How much do you think the stocks will go up in the direction that you want? This will tell you how much reward you can make in the process. Your research should tell you a reasonable price that you can get for the stocks, so consider that when you pick out an entry point. It would be nice to get a deep discount on a stock, but that is just not possible in these kinds of trades most of the time. You should be able to tell what the low point, or even the average, is for this stock, and then your goal is to purchase close to that.

Before you enter into the trade, it is time to make some decisions on what your stop-loss points are. You need to have one in place for how you will get out if things take a turn for the worse and you start losing profit. And you need one in place for when you start making profits.

With swing trading, you will often jump in early and get some stocks for a discount before others do, and before a big event. This event may be temporary, and the price of the stock may neutralize a bit and can even go back down. This is why the stop loss for profits is important. It will make sure that you take the profits and get out of the market before you lose everything that you earned.

A stop loss to prevent you from losing too much money is important here as well. this will ensure that when the trend goes opposite of what you had estimated, you will get out of the game and limit your risks. You can decide how much risk you are willing to take, and how much money you would be willing to lose. But the best bet is to set this ahead of time before the emotions can get into the game and mess up your plans.

Most brokers online will make it simple to do this process. You can look up the stock, click on a button that says buy or purchase. When you get there, decide how many of the stock you would like to purchase. This depends on how much money you are willing to invest and how much the stock costs. Agree to the market value and click submit.

The trade is going to usually happen in real-time, though if there is a lot of volatility or something else going on, then it can take a few minutes to finish up. Once that is done, then you are in the market. It is important that you take the time to watch the market and see what it does. The market will have a lot of ups and downs over the next few days, so don't worry if you see some profits lost during this because it will most likely bounce up unless there is a big change in the market or in the company.

You should know about when the big event is going to happen that you want to capitalize on, so that should help here. But there can be some unexpected changes that creep up on a regular basis, so it is always a good idea to watch the stocks and see what they do. If something goes the wrong way or doesn't act how you thought it would, then it is time to get out of the market and try something new.

The goal here, if you did all of the research well and you made sure that your risk and reward were at a good ratio, then you will be able to get out of the market at the right time to make some good profits. You will not get rich off one trade though, even with the possibility of making some good money, so take that off the table right now. Thinking about this logically and understanding that you need to put in some work and do the swing trading many times to become rich, will help to keep your emotions in check and will make your trades more successful.

And that is the process that you need to follow to get started with swing trading! You will just rinse and repeat, doing this over and over again, and putting in the right safeguards to make sure that your money is as safe and possible through all of this. When that comes together, you can start to make a good profit with swing trading, and you will get a whole lot better at it in the process as well.

CHAPTER 3

THE TECHNICAL ANALYSIS

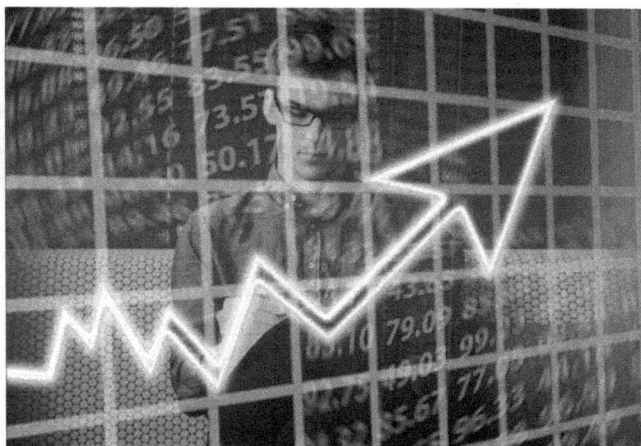

There are two main types of analysis that we can do when it is time to enter into swing trading, or really any kind of trading for that matter. We have mentioned them a little bit before and introduced them as the technical analysis and fundamental analysis. Now it is time for us to go into some more details about what these are and how they work, so we can utilize them for some of our needs as we enter into the market. You will see that these two types of analysis peak out for any kind of investment that you do in the stock market or with other securities, so learning them now can help you if you decide to branch out to other types of investments later.

What Is Technical Analysis?

The first place to start here is looking at what technical analysis is all about. This is a strategy that we can use in order to take a look at some of our investments, evaluate them a bit, and then find the best opportunities to help us jump into the market and trade for a profit. These are usually found by analyzing some of the statistical trends on particular security gathered from the trading activity, such as the price movement and the volume.

This basically means that we are going to use a lot of charts and graphs to help us make some decisions on what will happen with a particular security. We can look these over and determine whether the stock or security will go up or down, how far in either direction it will go, and whether we should purchase or sell based on those trends. It doesn't usually take into account any of the other factors about the company itself, assuming that the charts and graphs will tell us the information that we need.

Unlike what we see with a fundamental analysis, which we will explore in more detail in the next chapter, this analysis is going to try and focus on the price or the volume of the stock and see what will happen next. These tools of technical analysis are going to be used as a way to figure out what the supply and demand for the security are and how that is going to change the price. This gives us the implied volatility as well.

This seems like a lot, but by carefully exploring and studying the charts that we are able to find, it is possible to see how this works and when we should make our trades. The technical analysis is often a good option to use in order to generate some trading signals for the short-term from a lot of tools during charting. But we can also use it to help improve the evaluation that we do with the strength of the security, or even the weakness of the security, based on the broader market or one of the sectors that go with it. This is very valuable information because it helps us to improve our estimations.

The technical analysis can be used on any and every security that you want, as long as that security has some historical trading data to go with it. This means that we are able to complete this technical analysis on anything that we want, including currencies, commodities, stocks, and futures, to name a few. We will work with stocks because that is the option that most people like to use when they enter into the stock market, but it is not the only choice out there.

To recap, there are a few things that we need to remember before we dive into the rest of this chapter. This includes:

1. Technical analysis is basically going to be a discipline of trading that is used in order to do an evaluation of investments and then identify some of the opportunities of trading based on

the price patterns and trends that we are able to see while looking at the charts

2. The technical analyst will believe that the activity and some of the price changes of the past will be able to tell them all they need to know about where the security will go in the future.

3. We can see that this is different than the fundamental analysis because we focus more on the charts, rather than on the fundamentals of the company itself.

The Basics of Technical Analysis

Another thing that we need to take a look at here is some of the basics that come with this technical analysis. This was a theory that was introduced as the Dow Theory by Charles Dow during the late 1800s. there are a number of important researchers out there who helped to add to the concepts we see in this theory to make sure that we are able to get the basics of it, and can use it properly. Then in our modern world, the technical analysis has seen some changes so that it can include so many different signals and patterns, hundreds of them by some estimates, though lots of research.

This type of analysis is going to work based on the assumption that trading activity from the past, and the changes in price from the past, of a security, can be really valuable indicators of the future movements in the price of that security when it is paired together with some of the other tradings and investing worlds.

There are a lot of people who will use this kind of technical analysis. For example, professionals in this will use the technical analysis along with some other forms of research in order to get the best results and make the best decisions. Retail traders are going to sometimes make decisions that are based right on the price of the charts that they get with that security and some other statistics. But if you go through and do this for a long time, you will find that technical and fundamental analysis should not be used on their own.

The Assumptions of the Technical Analysis

There are going to be two methods that we can use when it is time to analyze the securities that we want to work with, and when we make some good investment decisions. These include the technical analysis that we are talking about here and the fundamental analysis.

As a brief overview, the fundamental analysis is going to be when we look at the financials of the business, and some of their potential in order to really determine the fair value that the business has. And then we can make some decisions based on that. Then there is a technical analysis, which is going to have us look at a lot of the charts that we want to focus on to make some decisions. This one will assume that the price that is found in the charts will already show all of the information that we need to know about the company, and we can then focus on some of the statistical analysis of the price movements to make these decisions.

When we work with the technical analysis, it is going to try and understand some of the sentiments of the market that are found behind the trends in the price of that security. This is going to be one that will look for patterns and trends instead of looking and analyzing the fundamental attributes of the security.

here are a few important things that we need to remember when it comes to working with the technical analysis, and knowing how to make this work is going to be so important to our overall success. Some of the things that we need to consider to get the most out of the technical analysis include:

1.   The market already discounts everything

Those who follow this kind of analysis already believe that everything about the company, including market psychology, the various market factors that are out there, and some of the fundamentals of the company, are already reflected in the stock price. It assumes that we do not need to go through and do any more work than looking at the charts because this will tell us all that we need to know.

With this assumption in place, we just have one thing left to work on. We need to spend time analyzing the price movements, which we are going to be able to find inside some of the charts that we look through for that company. The technical analyst is going to look at this and see the price changes as the product of supply and demand for a certain stock that they are trying to look through on the market.

2.   The price will move on trends

In addition to what we have taken a look at above, the technical analysis is going to expect that the prices that happen with the stock, even some of the market movements that are random are going to exhibit a trend that we can follow, no matter what kind of time frame we are looking at. This is good news because we are able to look at a particular stock and notice when it is going to head up and when it will go down and can make some smart decisions along the way.

The idea here is that the price of the stock, no matter what stock you are working with, is most likely to go on with a past trend rather than having it move erratically. There may be some exceptions for a short amount of time, but for the most part, the stock price is going to stick to the trend. Most technical trading strategies that you will want to work with are completely based on this assumption.

3.   History is going to repeat

The third thing that we need to look at when it is time to work on technical analysis is that history is more likely to repeat itself. Technical analysts believe that history is going to repeat itself over and over again. The price movements that we can look at are repetitive in nature, and this is because of market psychology, which is actually more predictable than we may think.

It is often going to be based on the emotions of people, like fear and excitement. When people are excited about a stock, they are more likely to purchase it. When they are scared about the price dropping or something happening on the stock, then they will sell.

The technical analysis is going to work with chart patterns to help analyze these emotions and then the market movements that come with it, to make sure they can learn more about the trends that may show up. While there are a lot of forms that come with technical analysis and why this method has been around for over 100 years, they are still really relevant because they are good at showing us some patterns that come in the price movements, and since they repeat themselves, it is a good thing to look at.

How to Use the Technical Analysis

This kind of analysis will work on forecasting some of the movements in the price of any security that you can work with, and it is often going to be subject to the forces of demand and supply. In fact, there are some who see this as a process that helps them to see the supply and demand forces based on the movements in the market price of that security. Often this is something that will apply back to the changes in prices, but some analysts are more likely to track some other numbers along the way than the price, including the open interest figures, and trading volume if they needed to.

When you look through any industry, there will be hundreds of signals and patterns, and researchers are always developing some more to help support the trading that uses this. The technical analysts will work with more than one type of trading system in order to make it easier to forecast and trade on these movements in price.

Some of the indicators that we can use will be focused on identifying the current trend in the market, including some of the resistance and support areas, while others are going to be focused more on figuring out how strong a trend is and how likely it is that the trend will continue into the future. There are a lot of technical indicators that we are able to focus on, along with some good charting patterns that we can add in, and these include options like the moving averages, channels, trendlines, and momentum indicators.

To keep it simple, a technical analyst will take a look at a lot of indicators to help them out, and some of the ones that you will get really familiar with as we go through this process include:

1. The price trends
2. Support and resistance levels
3. Chart patterns
4. Moving averages
5. Oscillators
6. Momentum and volume indicators

These are just a few of the options that we are able to work with based on how the market is going, how your stock is behaving, and even based on what seems to work the best for your needs. You may want to try out a few of these to figure out which ones seem to give you the best results when you trade and work from there.

Some Limitations That Come With Technical Analysis

There are a lot of options that come with using the technical analysis, and this is one of the best options to make sure that we can get some profits when we work on swing trading. But this is not the option that you will want to use all of the time. There are a few limitations that show up when we want to work with this type of analysis.

Some researchers and analysts worry that this is not going to work the way that we would like when it is time to start investing. The EMH will show us why we should not expect any kind of actionable information inside the price and volume data in the past of the stock. However, with this same kind of reasoning, business fundamentals should not provide any kind of information that we can act on either. These points of view are going to be referred back to the weak form and the semi-strong form of the EMH.

Another issue that can show up when we use the technical analysis is that history is never going to repeat itself the exact same way all the time. This means that the price patter study that we do with the technical analysis is kind of dubious and may not provide the results that we are hoping for. It is often better to see the prices modeled by assuming a random walk. Whether you think that history will repeat itself will make a big difference in whether you will actually use this method or not.

Then there is also a third criticism that shows up with this as well. this one talks about how the technical analysis can work in some instances, but only because it fulfills the self-fulfilling prophecy. For example, the technical trader is going to place a stop-loss order below what is the 200-day moving average of a certain company. If there are a lot of traders who have done the same thing and then the stock does go to this point, there will all of a sudden be a huge number of orders to sell things, and that will push the price of the stock back down. This basically just confirms the movement that the traders were anticipating in the first place.

Then, there are other traders who will see some of these price decreases and then work on selling the position they have, which is going to be there to reinforce the strength of the trend that we see. This type of short-term selling pressure is kind of the same idea, but it is not going to have much bearing on where the price of the asset will be in a few weeks or even a few months from now.

Basically, if there are enough traders in the market who use the same signals,then it is possible that they will have the right amount of pressure to cause the movement they were working with through the signal. But over the long-term, this group will not be enough to drive the price and this will not work out as well for them as they had hoped.

Is the Technical Analysis of a Good Strategy?

There are a lot of good reasons to use the technical analysis, but there are also a lot of researchers and analysts who advise not to use it at all this can make it confusing to someone who is new to this and who would wonder whether it is actually going to help them to see some results with trading.

There are a ton of swing traders who work with this kind of strategy. It is easy to work with and allows us to work with some of the trends and the charts that go with the stock or another security that we want to use. And that is all that you need to focus on. And since you are not planning on keeping this position for the long-term, and your goals are to sell it off within a few weeks, often the fundamentals are not that important, and you will get all of the information you need from the trade from your charts and graphs.

For some of the most successful swing traders, using a combination of the technical and the fundamental analysis will be the best way to make sure that you are successful with your trades. This allows you to learn more about what works best with the trends of the company and how their prices have gone up and down while also taking a look at how the company is doing financially and looking at some of the news that surrounds it as well before making your decisions.

Combining the technical and the fundamental analysis is one of the best ways to make sure that you get the full picture of a stock and the company that controls it as well. And the more information that you have about that company and about that stock, the easier it can be to make predictions on where the price will move in the future, and whether this is a good option to help you be successful and take home a profit.

The technical analysis is a pretty easy strategy to understand. You will take a look at a lot of the charts and graphs that come with the stock or the security that you want to work on, and then you make some decisions on where the price of the stock will go in the future. Sometimes we add in fundamental analysis, or at least pay some attention to the news, to figure out if there will be some big spikes, either up or down, that may not show up in the charts and other research that we do.

The idea with the technical analysis is that we will focus more on the price movements and the idea of supply and demand. Many professional traders will use more than one method to make sure they pick the right stocks, and you can too. Later on, we will look at a few of the strategies that we can utilize that are all considered technical analysis tools, and that will help us to know what signs and signals we need to look at before making some of our purchasing decisions.

CHAPTER 4

HOW THE FUNDAMENTAL ANALYSIS IS DIFFERENT

Once we have had some time to learn more about the technical analysis and how that will work, it is time for us to move on to learn more about the fundamental analysis and how we can use this for our needs. This option is not going to spend as much time looking at the charts and graphs that come with some of the stocks and securities that we want to use. It may glance at them a bit, but it focuses more on some of the options that will help to determine whether the company that is under the stock, is secure and has some good things behind it. then the analyst will determine whether the current price of the stock is undervalued or overvalued based on that information.

There are a lot of parts that have to come together in order to work on the fundamental analysis. And many will agree that using this method is a lot more in-depth and harder to work on compared to the technical analysis that we talked about before. This should not deter you at all because it is a great strategy that can help you get good deals on some of the stocks or securities that you want to use. It is just a little bit different. Let's dive in and look at how we can use this.

What Is Fundamental Analysis?

The first thing that we need to take a look at here is the fundamental analysis. This is going to be a method that a trader is able to use in order to measure out the intrinsic value of security because we will examine some of the different factors that we can see that may influence the price of the stock, including the financial and the economic factors.

A fundamental analyst will study anything that is able to affect the value of the security, including some of the macroeconomic factors like how the economy is doing and some of the conditions of the particular industry you are focusing on, all the way to some of the microeconomic factors, like how effective the management of the company can be.

The end goal of doing this is to come up with a number that the investor is going to use for what they think the price of the security should be. They can then take that and compare it to the current price of that security to figure out whether the security is undervalued or overvalued. This makes it easier to figure out whether the trader should dive in and purchase the security or not.

This is a method of analyzing a stock or another security, and it works in contrast to the technical analysis that we were talking about in the previous chapter. This one looks more at the daily running around the business, and some of the outside factors that can influence the business, rather than worrying about the historical data and how the price will move based on these trends.

There are a few points that we can keep in mind here to make sure that we understand how this is supposed to work and how we can ensure that we get the best results will include the following:

1. This kind of analysis is going to be the method that we can use to figure out the fair market value of a stock and then decide whether the current price is above or under that.

2. The trader who uses this option will search around for some stocks that are currently

trading at prices that are lower or higher than what their real value is all about.

3. If the fair market value is higher than what the price of the market is, then this shows us that the stock is being undervalued in the market right now. It is recommended to purchase the stock when this happens because it is likely that the market will go up, and we can make some profit in the process.

Understanding How the Fundamental Analysis Works

Now we need to take a closer look at how the fundamental analysis can be used for some of your trading needs. All analysis of the stock market will try to figure out whether the value of a security is valued well or not within the whole market. Fundamental analysis will often be done from the macro to the micro perspective so that we can better find some of the securities that are not being priced well, or the right way, in the market.

Analysts who use this option are going to study many different things to figure this out, including how the economy is working and doing, and then the strength of the industry that the specific security is in right then. When this is all done, the trader will move on to looking at the performance of that individual company and how it compares to some of the other companies in the industry. This helps them to arrive at the market value that is fair for that stock.

This kind of analysis is going to make use of lots of public data to help evaluate the value of the stock or any other security that you want to work with. For example, it is common for an investor can perform fundamental analysis on the value of the bond, and they will do it by looking at the economic factors that are out there, including some of the interest rates available, and then how the state of the economy is behaving at the time. Then we are able to study the information about the bond issuer, including some changes that may show up in the credit rating of the company.

For stocks, fundamental analysis is going to look at a lot of different things to figure out the value of the company and how much potential that is there for the company to grow in the future. For example, we would want to look at things like the profit margins, the return on equity, the future growth, earnings, and revenues, along with a few other options, to figure all of this out. The good news is that while there are a lot of options out there that we need to explore and look at, all of this data is available in the financial statements that the company has to release to the public so you can get it easily.

Fundamental Analysis and Investing

There are a lot of times when the fundamental analysis is going to be used in investing, especially in the stock market. In this one, the trader will take some time to create their own model to determine the value of the company based on the data that is publicly out there for them. The value they come up with is only an estimate, and the opinion of the trader, of what the price of the company's shares should be. Then they can compare it to the price that the shares are currently trading out. Some analysts could call this estimated price the intrinsic value of the company.

If a trader comes in and finds that the stock's value should be significantly higher than the current price of the market of the stock, then they may publish a buy rating for the stock. This is going to be the recommendation to investors who follow that analyst. If the trader then goes through and sees things the opposite way and find a lower intrinsic value than the current price of the market, the stock is considered overvalued, and then they will issue out a recommendation to sell.

Investors who decide to follow some of these recommendations will expect that they would then be able to buy stocks that are favorable, and that will provide them with some profitability as well. Many times beginners are going to look at what the analysts say and follow all that, but it is possible to go through and do the analysis on your own and come to your own conclusions as well.

The Difference Between Qualitative and Quantitative Fundamental Analysis

One of the problems that will come with defining the word fundamentals is that it is possible that it will cover anything and everything that will relate back to the well-being economically of the company. They will include some obvious numbers like the profits and the revenue of the company, but it is possible that it can include a lot of other things, like the quality of the management of this company and the market share as well.

The good news here is that there are a lot of fundamental factors that we can include, but we are able to group them into two broad categories to make it easier to understand what is going on here. And these two categories are going to include qualitative and quantitative options. The financial meaning that we see with the terms is going to be similar to their standard definitions, but to review, the definitions that we will use include:

1. Quantitative: This means that the item is capable of being expressed or measured in numerical terms.

2. Qualitative: This is something that is based or related to the quality of the character of something, rather than the quantity or the size of it.

With this as our context, the quantitative fundamentals that we will want to use are more about the hard numbers. These are going to be some of the characteristics that we can measure the business. This is why we will see the biggest sources of this data type will be in the financial statements. You can also go through and look at the assets, profits, and revenue and get the measurements with great precision.

Then we can look at some of the qualitative fundamentals, which are considered less tangible through this. They could include things like the quality of the top executives of the company, the recognition of the brand name, the patents, and more. These are a bit harder to look through when we focus on the company, but they are still important and have some value that we need to look at.

We need to consider here that neither of the two fundamentals is not going to be seen as more important than the other one. In fact, most people who work with these will consider both of them at the same time to make some of their decisions. Let's take a look at some of the factors that we can consider with both of these and learn how this can be beneficial to our needs.

The Qualitative Fundamentals

There are a lot of things that we can consider when we are working through all of this and figuring out the qualitative fundamentals along the way. There are four main fundamentals that we will want to take a look at when we focus on the qualitative fundamentals, and these include:

The model of the business. With this one, we are going to spend some time looking at what the company does. This can be harder to pin down than it seems something. If there is a company that will sell fast-food chicken, is it making its money that way, or is it working on royalties and some fees from franchisees? These are things that we need to consider before we make our decisions.

Then we can look at some of the competitive advantages that we are able to work with on that company. The long-term success that a company has is driven quite a bit by how well it can be competitive in the industry, and how they can keep this edge. The more powerful this advantage, the safer the business is, and it can keep others at bay while the company will enjoy some profits and growth in the process. When a company is able to add on some of this kind of competitive advantage, then the shareholders are going to do well and can see some good profits for years to come.

Another thing that we need to take a look at its management. Some believe that this is actually the most important thing that we need to consider when investing in the company. This makes a lot of sense if we think it through. Even some of the best models in business will be doomed if the people who run and lead the company do not execute the plan well or don't take care of the company.

Of course, as someone who is simply investing in the company, it is hard to go in and meet and see how the managers are doing, you can still take a look at the corporate website, check out the resumes of those who are in charge, and read the news to see what is going on with the company. This can help you to take a look at how the management is doing and whether they will continue to do the great work that you need in the future.

And the fourth thing that we are going to take a look at is something known as corporate governance. This will include all of the policies that are found in the company that will tell us more about the responsibilities and the relationships between the stakeholders, the directors, and the management. These policies are going to be determined and defined right from the company charter and some of their bylaws, along with some of the corporate laws and regulations that they need to focus on.

You want to do business and do some of the tradings with a company that is run in an ethical manner, one that is fair, transparent, and as efficient as possible. If any of these are gone, then you could be in trouble when you try to invest. You should take some particular note of whether the management respects the rights of the shareholders and their interests as well. check to see whether the communication they have with the shareholders is understandable, clear, and transparent. If you do not get what is being said, there is usually a good reason for this, and that can be a big red flag along the way.

The final thing that we are going to work with this one is the industry that the company is in. you can also look at information like the business cycles, regulation, competition, the growth of the whole industry, the market share among all the firms in the industry, and the customer base. Learning about the whole industry and then comparing it back to the company you want to invest in can make it easier to see the financial health of the company.

The Quantitative Fundamentals

Since we have had some time to look more at some of the qualitative fundamentals, we need to look at some more of the quantitative options as well. these are going to focus a bit more on some of the financials that are found with the company to make sure that it is steady and secure. You don't want to get into an investment and then find out that the company just filed bankruptcy, and your investment is gone.

This one will work a lot with the financial statements of the company. These statements are going to be the medium used by a company to show all the information that investors, current and potential, will need about its financial performance. Followers of this kind of analysis will take a look at this data and use it to make some of the investment decisions.

There are a number of financial statements and more that we can look at depending on the strategy that we want to use. The three that you should definitely take some time on and explore, no matter what other strategies you work on, include the cash flow statements, the balance sheets, and the income statements.

First on the list is the balance sheet. This is an important financial statement of a company that will take a look at all the equity, liabilities, and assets of a company at one particular point in time. These three things will change on a regular basis, so that is why we must remember that it is up to date based on when the report was generated. The balance sheet is going to be named this way because it will have the financial structure balances of the company listed out with the following formula:

Assets = Liabilities + Shareholders/Equity

The assets are going to show us all the resources that the business is in control over or owns at that particular period of time. This can include many things like buildings, machinery, inventory, and cash. These are important to help us see how well the company is doing overall.

Then we can move over to the other part of the equation. This is going to show us the total of the value of the financing the company may be using, and that is still owed, in order to get those assets. Financing is going to come as a result of equity or liabilities. Liabilities are going to represent the debt, which the company has to pay back at some point, and then the equity is going to show the total value of money that the owners have already added back to the business. This equity can include the retained earnings or the profit that was made in the previous years.

This is an important thing to look through. While it is not a bad thing for a company to have some debt in order to purchase the machinery and the other items that they need, it can get out of hand. If the debts are too high and it seems like the company is drowning and not going to be able to pay back those debts, then this is a red flag that should keep you away from investing in them.

Once we are all done with the balance sheet, we are able to move on to what is known as the income statement. While the balance sheet is a good snapshot to tell us a lot about the finances of the business, the income statement is going to measure the performance of the company over a time frame. So, the balance sheet is usually over a month or a day, and then the income statement is going to be moreover a quarter or a whole year so you can see how they handle their finances and more throughout the time.

The income statement is a good option to take a look at along the way, and you should not focus on the fundamental analysis without looking at this. You will find that it is going to present you with a lot of information about the profits, expenses, and revenues that the company was able to generate over a certain time period by doing their normal business operations.

And the final of the three financial statements that you need to take a look at to complete your fundamentals analysis here is the statement of cash flows. This is going to be a record that we can look over to see the cash inflows and outflows of business over some period of time. This is usually going to look at a few important cash related activities, including:

1. The operating cash flow: This is the cash the business is able to generate from their daily business operations.

2. Cash from financing: This is going to be all the cash that is received or paid from issuing and borrowing funds.

3. Cash from investing: This is going to be the cash that would be used to invest in assets, and sometimes it is the proceeds from the sale of other long-term assets, equipment, and businesses.

This statement is an important one to spend some time on because it is really hard for a business to go in and manipulate at all. There are a lot of accountants who can become aggressive here and manipulate the earnings hat they have, but it is tough to fake cash in the bank. For this reason, this is going to be a good conservative measure that we are able to look at to see more about the performance of the company.

The Idea of Intrinsic Value

One of the primary assumptions that we can make when it comes to working with the fundamental analysis is that the current price that we can see for the stock on the stock market is not really telling us much about the company and what it is really worth. A second assumption that will come up is that the valet hat we get from the fundamental data of the company is going to help us to see the true value of the stock, and then we can make some better choices based on that.

It is common for analysts to refer to this hypothetical true value as something known as the intrinsic value. However, we have to note that using the phrase of intrinsic value means something different when we work with stock valuation than it will mean with other choices like options trading. When we talk about options trading, we are going to work with a standard calculation to figure out our intrinsic value. For the stock market, we would use a variety of complex models to get the intrinsic value of the stock. There is not a single formula that is accepted and used all over for how to find this intrinsic value.

For example, let's say that we find a stock for one company that is trading at $20. We do some of the research that is required for fundamental analysis and determine that the stock should be worth at least $24. Then there is another analyst who comes in and thinks that the value of that same stock should be closer to $26. Many investors here would consider the average of the estimates and then assume that the value is closer to $25 based on this. Often the investor would see these as relevant estimates because they want to purchase stocks that are trading at prices that are significantly below some of these intrinsic values.

We can take this the other way as well. If you find that there is a stock listed out at $20, but your research and your own fundamental analysis says that it is worth $15, then this is not a good one to go with. If the market catches up with it, then the price of the stock will go down, and you would lose money if you purchased at the $20 mark.

This will lead us to the third assumption that we need to make about the fundamental analysis. With this one, in the long run, the stock market is going to always meet up with the fundamentals. It may take some time, and we don't really know how long that can be, whether it is days or years or some other time frame, but at some point, this will happen.

And that is what the fundamental analysis is all about. When we are able to focus on a particular business, then we are able to estimate the intrinsic value of a firm and find all of the opportunities to purchase that at a discount. The investment is going to pay off sometime in the future when the market finally catches up with those fundamentals.

Criticisms of This Method

While we are here, we need to take a look at some of the criticisms that come with this analysis. One of the main criticisms that we will see with this kind of analysis will come with two groups of things; the proponents who want to work with the technical analysis, and then those who believe in the efficient market hypothesis.

First, we will dive into those who like to work with the technical analysis. This is the other method that we talked about, one that relies heavily on all of the charts and the graphs that you are able to find, and then you make your decisions based on that. Since the fundamental analysis isn't going to spend as much time on the charts and graphs, these are really different options to work with.

One of the basic ideas that come with this technical analysis is that the stock market is already going to take into account all of the fundamentals and that it discounts everything. All the news that is publicly available to us about the company will be reflected in the price of the stock. This is why the fundamental analysis would not work, according to these traders. The price movements of the stock, in their opinion, will provide us with more insight compared to looking at the underlying fundamentals.

Then we need to look a bit more at something known as the efficient market hypothesis. Followers of this are usually going to be in some kind of disagreement with both of the analysis types that we have talked about. This may sound confusing, but they take a different approach to look at the market and figuring out what works and what does not.

This hypothesis is going to state that it is pretty much impossible to beat out the market through technical analysis or the fundamental analysis. Since the market has already priced out the stocks as efficiently as possible, and it does this on an ongoing basis, any opportunities for excess returns are going to be whittled away by all of the participants in the market. This means that it is almost impossible for anyone to really outperform the market when it comes to working with it over the long term.

All of these methods have their merits, and it really depends on what we are trying to accomplish and what or end goals are all about. When we are able to look through the documents and the financial statements of a company, we can sometimes find some hidden gems that will tell us more about the process and all that it entails as well. but sometimes, this is not going to provide us with the right information and technical analysis, with us pouring over charts and learning about the markets that way will be the right method.

Often combining the two of these together will be the right answer and can provide us with a good way to figure out which stocks we want to work with overall. This can make life a bit easier to work with this method, but you have to choose which one is the best for your needs as well. both can be efficient for swing trading, so go with the one that makes the most sense for you.

CHAPTER 5

SWING TRADING WITH DIFFERENT SECURITIES

Before we go into some of the basics of the strategies that we are able to work with as we go through this process, we need to make sure that we understand some of the different securities that you can use when it is time to start swing trading. You can technically work with any kind of security that you would like when it is time to start swing trading, though we did spend quite a bit of time looking at how to do this with stocks because that is the most common option. Let's take a look at a few of the other choices that you can make when it is time to start trading with the various securities that are available for you.

Swing Trading With Stocks

The first option that we can take a look at is the stocks. This is the most common instrument to use when we want to trade, especially with swing trading, because it is the least complicated choice out there. But we need to take a look at this a bit more. First, what is a stock?

This is basically a security that will help to show what percentage of ownership you have in a company. And it will entitle the owner of the stock a proportion of the assets and profits of the corporation. This is equal to how much stock you own. These units will be known as shares.

The stocks are going to be purchased and then sold on the stock exchanges, though there are times when a private sale can happen, and we will find these stocks are the foundation of the portfolio for most people. These transactions do have to meet up with some regulations from the government to ensure that an investor is protected from those who try to defraud them. You can also purchase them from most of the online stock brokers who are out there.

So, how do you get one of these stocks? It is common for companies to issue, or sell, stocks to help them to raise funds to operate their business. The holder of the stock, which would be you if you purchase one during swing trading, has basically purchased a piece of the corporation, and, depending on what kind of shares they hold onto, they could also have some kind of claim on the earnings and assets of the company.

What this means is that the shareholder is technically an owner of that company, along with others who own the stock as well. ownership is going to be based on how many of these shares you own relative to how many outstanding shares you have. Those who have 10,000 shares would have a higher ownership in the company compared to those who have 100 shares, for example.

Keep in mind with this one, that you do not actually own the company. You will own the shares that the company issues. But the corporation is a special thing, and by law, they are treated as legal persons. This means that they are able to file taxes, can borrow, can own some property, and can be sued just like a regular person. The idea that the corporations that are out there are a person means that it is able to own their own assets. So all of the chairs and equipment and computers in the company will belong to it and not to its shareholders.

This is an important distinction because it shows us hat the company is separated legally from the property of the shareholders, which helps to limit how much liability of the company and the shareholder, so that is a good thing for you as well. for example, if the company goes bankrupt, a judge can order all of the assets to be sold, but you will never have your assets taken from you if something goes wrong with the company.

As a swing trader, you will not hold onto the stocks for very long. But it is still important to understand some of the basics that go with this and what the stocks mean if you are using them for trading and other purposes. They are easy to purchase and sell during normal business hours on the stock exchange, which can make them an attractive choice if you are working as a swing trader.

Swing Trading With Options

Another choice that we can make when we want to work with swing trading is something known as options trading. These are slightly different than the stock market, though there are a few parts that you will recognize as your work with this. To start, options are going to be financial instruments that are derivatives that are then based on the value of the underlying securities, including stocks and other options.

The options will offer the buyer the opportunity to sell or purchase, based on the type of contract that you hold onto, the underlying asset. Unlike what we can do with the futures, the person who has the contract does not have to sell or buy that asset if they choose not to. There are two types of options that we are able to work with as well. The first choice that you have the call options will allow the holder to purchase the asset at a stated price within a specific timeframe. The put options will allow the holder to sell the asset at a stated price within a specific timeframe.

Both of those contracts will have an expiration date by which the holder will be able to exercise that option if they would like. The price that is stated on the option is called the strike price, and it is common that these options will be sold and bought through retail or online brokers in most cases.

That was an introduction to what options are about, but how should we work with these options if we choose to use this for swing trading? Options are a really versatile financial product to work with. The contracts are going to involve a buyer and a seller. The buyer will come in and pay an options premium for the rights that are granted through the contract. Each call option will have a bullish buyer in them, and then the seller will be bearish. The put options will be the opposite of a bullish seller and a bearish buyer.

We will find that the options contracts will usually represent about 100 shares of the security that is under it, and then the buyer is able to pay a premium fee for each contract they want to work with. So, if you have an option that has the premium set to 35 cents for each control, if you purchased one of these options, which is 100 shares, it would cost you $35. Keep in mind that this is a really oversimplified method to work with, and it is likely that you will need to pay more than this to get things going.

The premium is something that all buyers will have to pay in order to get this started, and the amount that you pay is based on the strike price. Remember that the strike price is the price you pay for buying or selling the security until that expiration date that is set up on it. Another factor in the premium price that you will pay is the expiration date. If that date is close, then the price will be a bit lower, but if there is a lot of time for the underlying asset to make a move, then the price will be lower.

Traders and investors will be able to come in and choose whether to purchase or sell these options any time that they would like. And they may choose the options as their vehicle for investing for a number of reasons. First, speculating on these options will allow you to come in and hold a leveraged position on an asset at a lower cost compared to purchasing the direct shares of that asset. The investor will also have the choice to hedge or reduce some of the exposure that comes with their portfolio when they use this. And then, there are some situations where the option holder is able to generate income when they use these call options or work as an options writer.

The reason that people will choose to go with options is going to vary based on some of their own goals and what they hope to get out of the market in the process. You can choose to use this because it is seen as safer, the costs of joining are lower, and it can be a lot of fun. And it does work well with some of the swing tradings we have been talking about, so that is a great choice.

One thing that we need to discuss before we leave here and move on to some of the other choices you can make for swing trading is the idea that there are two types of options; the American options and the European options. The American options are the ones that you can exercise any time before the expiration date on the option. On the other hand, the European options are the ones that you have to hold onto until the expiration date, and then you can use them.

Swing Trading With Forex

Stocks and options are the two most likely choices that beginners with swing trading are going to make to help them get into the market and enjoy the results with some good profits. But there are other choices that can really open up some more doors to what you can do and can make the trading a bit more interesting in the process. In this section, we will take a bit of time to look at forex trading and how well this can work with some of your needs as a swing trader.

Forex is basically a trading method of foreign currency and exchange. It is the process of taking one currency and changing it over to another currency for a variety of reasons. If you have ever traveled to another country and used their money, or purchased something and had it shipped to you from Europe, then you have participated in the Forex market at some point. We can even use this as one of the methods to help us trade and get amazing results.

This is a really large market, which can be intimidating for someone who is just entering it and trying to find their way. according to a recent report that the Bank for International Settlements released, it is estimated that the Forex market has a trading volume of more than $5.1 trillion a day. That is an extraordinary amount.

To help us see whether this is the right investment vehicle for our needs, we need to look more at what the forex market entails. This is basically a market where we will exchange various types of currencies. Currencies are so important to many people around the world, even if you do not realize it at first. This is because we use currencies to help conduct some of the foreign trade and the business we want to accomplish. We use it on a daily basis, even if we are not trading on the forex market.

Let's say that you are living in the United States and choose to purchase a designer dress, or some other product from France, who relies on Euros while you rely on the USD. You or the company you purchase the dress from has to pay the French for the dress in Euros. And that means we need to bring into the game a U.S. importer who could help to exchange these and make sure that the person in France who made the dress is getting paid the right amount.

This is the same when we want to travel. We can come from any country in the world, but if we head to Egypt to take a look at some of the pyramids that are out there, then we need to make sure that we bring in the right currency, or we are out of luck. This is the most common way that we think about the forex market, as a way for us to exchange our money to go traveling and get it in the right currency for the area that we want to visit.

But there are a lot of options that we can use for this one, including spending our time investing in the market and exchanging one currency for another to make as much money as possible. This one is a bit more difficult because you have to know a lot about your own country of origin, as well as the country you would like to switch with. This is a bit more complicated since there are two variables, and you need to know the relations that happen between both. But if you do it well, it can help you make some good money.

One thing that is really unique about this kind of international market is that there isn't really a central marketplace for it like we see with stocks and options. Rather, currency trading is something that is done electronically and through a method known as over the counter. What this means for us is that all of the transactions happen between the traders in all parts of the world thanks to a vast computer network, rather than relying on one centralized exchange.

Another neat thing that you will notice with this one is that the market is open five and a half days a week and for 24 hours during those days, without a stop. This also allows us to trade all of the major currencies throughout the world, and you can use this in any of the major financial centers of the world. This means that even if the trading times end in the United States, you can then start it all anew in another market that is just opening. This can allow for a lot of activity no matter what time of day you decide to do your work.

This is a really unique way of handling some of the swing tradings that you would like to do, and it will bring in some new challenges that are a lot of fun. You have to consider how much risk you are willing to take, and whether or not you are able to keep up with the demand and all of the research that is necessary to do this for two currencies in comparison with one another. But for those who can do so successfully, the forex market can be a great place to do some trading.

Swing Trading With Futures
The final choice that we will take a look at when it is time to do some swing trading is known as futures.

Futures are going to be kind of similar to what we see with options, but with a few slight differences, that will be important if you decide to work with them. To start, these futures are basically going to be a derivative financial contract that will obligate those in the party to transact an asset at a predetermined future date and price. Here the buyer must purchase, or the seller has to sell the underlying asset at the set price, regardless of the current market price when the expiration date gets there.

With options, you can buy or sell, based on the contract, any time before the expiration date if you would like. And if things go south and don't work well for you, you can walk away and agree not to do anything with the contract. With the future, this is not true. You have to work with the contract and complete the right actions when the expiration date happens.

There are also a number of underlying assets that you can use here, including physical commodities and some other financial instruments that are wide open here as well. The contracts that come up here will show us how much of the underlying asset we work with, and they can be standardized in a way to make sure that we can trade well and easily on this kind of exchange as well.

Futures can also be known as futures contracts, and they allow the trader to lock in the price of the commodity or the underlying asset if they choose. These contracts will come to us with some expiration dates and a set price that will be known from the start. Futures are going to be known based on when they expire. For example, a December Gold futures contract will be done in December. The term here is going to help show the overall market in most cases. However, there are also a lot of types of these contracts that you can choose from including:

1. Commodity futures. These would include options like wheat, corn, natural gas, and crude oil.

2. Stock index futures like the S&P 500 index.

3. Precious metals that would include silver and gold

4. Currency futures including those for the USD< Euro, and the British pound.

5. Any U.S. Treasury futures for bonds and a few other products as well.

As we mentioned before, there are a few differences between futures and options, so we need to know how these are the same and different, so we need to consider that before choosing either. However, even with some of the issues and restrictions that come with this, there are a lot of benefits that come with it, including:

1. Investors are able to use these kinds of contracts to help them speculate on the direction in the price of an asset that is underlying their contract.

2. Companies are able to hedge the price of their raw materials or products that they already sell from some bad movements in the price.

3. These contracts may only require us to come up with a fraction of the contract amount, or a deposit, with the broker before we can get into the game.

There are some risks to working with this, of course. It is possible that you can go into this and lose more than the initial amount that you put down since futures will work with lots of leverage. Investing in a futures contract can cause a company that is hedged to miss out on some of the price movements that are more favorable. And then there is the idea of margin. This is a great thing in some cases but can be bad in others. It means that all of your gains are amplified, but your losses will be as well.

As we can see, there are a lot of choices that we are able to choose from when we wan to get started with swing trading. And all of them can provide us with some amazing benefits and can be a great way to make some money in the process. Do your research and figure out which one is the best for your needs.

CHAPTER 6

THE SWING TRADING STRATEGIES TO HELP YOU WIN

Now that we have had a lot of time to look at what swing trading is all about and how great it can be to work with this method of investing, it is time to take this a little bit further and look more at some of the strategies that we can use to really take our swing trading and make it as effective as possible. These strategies can all work in certain types of trades, and it depends on what you are the most comfortable with and how the market is behaving. Learning at least a few of them and gaining some confidence when using them will make a world of difference in how well you can make this happen. Let's dive in and look at some of the best options that you can go with when it is time to start swing trading

The Hull Moving Average Strategy

This is going to be a method that you can use that is completely based on the hull moving average indicator. If you have never heard about this, it is a moving average indicator that is smooth and will move

240

really fast. This is going to be a good thing because it is able to eliminate any of the lag that shows up in your work and can improve the smoothing all at the same time. What this means for us is that it is reactive to the price action as we go through with this.

There are two main ways that we are able to use this hull moving average to help us to purchase or sell something in the market. Some of these include:

1. We can look at the change of the slope. When this happens, then we know that it is time to get ready to purchase or sell our security.

2. If we see that the slope is going up, then it is time to purchase you can enter right then with the market order, or you can place your own buy stop pending order that is a few pips above the high of that new candlestick that should start to form and will cause your slow to go up. Make sure that this happens after the candlestick has time to close up.

3. If you see that the other slope is happening and it starts to go down, then it is time to prepare yourself to sell. You can either do this with a sell market order, or you can place your own sell stop pending order, as long as you do this somewhere between one to two pips under the low of your candlestick that is causing the slope of your hull to point down.

That is just one of the methods that you are able to use. It is also possible to work with something known as the Hull Moving Average Crossovers or the HMA. This one is going to be a fairly typical situation with a few of the other moving averages so you can check your work if you need it. Some of the steps that we can take to work with this method includes:

1. If you see that the faster HMA crosses the slower one to the upside, then this is a good sign that you are working with an uptrend.

2. If the faster HMA is able to cross the slower own going down, then this is a good sign that we are in a downtrend.

3. So what we want to do is wait around a bit for some of these HMA crossovers to happen, and then it is time to enter our buy or our sell order

4. If we are working with the setup to buy, we can either enter our own market order to place our own buy stop order. If we do this on our own, then it has to be done about one to two pips above the high candlestick that forms and will confirm the crossover. You can then place the stop loss in here as well, which will need to be around 5 pips below the low that you want.

5. For a sell setup, we are going to take the steps above and pretty much turn them around a bit to get our results. You would first enter into a sell market order, or you can do it yourself and work with a sell stop order hat is about one to two pips below the low of your candlestick that

will confirm the crossover. Then it is time to take that stop loss and place it about five pips above the high that comes with your candlestick.

And that is all that you need to work in order to make this strategy work. If you already know how to work with some of the basics of reading graphs and understanding what they say, then you will be set to go when it is time to work on this one as well. it is as simple as that and can work whether the market is going up or down, ensuring that you can keep on swing trading and getting the best results.

The ABCD Pattern

Another option that is really nice if you are into swing trading as a beginner is the ABCD pattern. This one is going to start us off with an upward move that is really strong. When this happens, you have a lot of buyers who are aggressively purchasing stock from point A, and then they will constantly bring in some new highs for that day, which will be point B. it is important to try and get in at B and trade here. But you do not want to chase the trade at all because B is usually higher than what the price is in the first place. Plus, this point is at a part where it is hard to know where to place the stop loss, and you do not want to get into a trade without this.

When you see that Point B shows up, the traders who have already gone in and purchased the stock at point A that we talked about earlier, will then start to sell off their stocks. This will not all happen at once, but it will slowly happen as a few decide to take the profits and call it good. This is not the time where you should enter the trade because it is hard to know when and where that pullback is going to happen.

If you are able to see that there is a bottom to this and the price just doesn't seem to go any further than it, then this is your point C. The security has found its support level, and you can go in and start planning the trade that you would like to use. If you get in at the right time and plan all of this out well, then you should be able to make a good amount of profit in the process.

This is a simple strategy that we are able to work with, which is why we are introducing it to you as a beginner. It is easy to understand and follow, and you won't feel as lost and confused along the way as some others may when they work on this one. There are a number of steps that we will have to use when we want to see this one work, and some of the steps will include:

- When you take a look through the scanner that you have set up, and you are looking for a stock, you want to look for one that is going o surge up from its original point A. You want it to get to a new high for that day. This is going to be point B.

- When these forms, you need to start paying attention. If you see that the new price is then going to become the support, and it goes up even more from there, then that is going to be point C. Be careful when you take a look at this because you have to wait for the right signs, rather than making assumptions and entering the market too soon.

- After you see the Point C showing up, you need to watch the stock carefully through this kind of consolidation period. From the information that you are able to gather at this time, you can then choose the right share size that you are comfortable with trading. You also need to spend this time looking for the stop and exit strategy that you would like to work with.

- When you see that the price is holding onto that support at point C, you should enter a trade at a point that is on or close to point C. The goal here is that your chosen security is going to move up to a new support point, known as point D, if not even higher.

- To work with this strategy, you want to have the stop loss end up at point C. If there is any time of the day where the price goes lower than your set point C, then you need to sell your stock and accept any losses that occur. The closer you can purchase the stock to that point C, the better with this strategy so that you can make sure your losses aren't too high.

- If you see that this stock continues to go higher, you will want to sell about half the position when it gets to point D. You can then move your stop higher to your entry point to help you make a profit.

- As soon as you see that the target is hit, or you see that the price is losing steam, even if it doesn't reach the goal, then you should sell the remaining shares that you have. When the price gets to a new low, this shows that the buyers are exhausted, and the trend will go backward.

There are a few steps that we need to follow to make this one work for our needs, but it is still a relatively simple process that even you as a beginner will be able to use and follow. However, to make it work as effectively as you would like, and to make sure that you can earn some profits from it, then you must have some patience. It is important with this one to only enter the markets at the right times, and to not get overly excited here, or you will end up losing a lot of money in the process.

Of course, we have to use some other caution here and be careful while watching the stock while you are in the trade, or you could miss out on a few things and lose a lot of money. It is possible that this trend can turn on you and start to go in a different direction than what you were planning, which is going to make it more difficult to work with and can cut into some of the profits that you want to make. But as a beginner who is looking to find a method to use that is simple and easy, then this is a good one to get started with.

The Shoulders and Head Patterns

Now it is time for us to move on to our third option to see how we are able to really make sure that we get some good results with our trading, and this is the head and shoulders pattern. This is a type of formation that you can notice on your graphs and charts that kind of looks like a baseline with three individual peaks. The two that fall on the outside should be similar in height, and then the one that falls right in the middle of them needs to be the highest.

This is a strategy that we are able to use in order to figure out if there is a trend reversal about to happen in the market or not. You can use it to see whether the trend reversal is bullish or bearish in nature as well. the pattern that you work with is going to include and be formed in three main parts, and all of them need t to be there to make sure that this trend works. The three parts that we need to spend some of our time on here to be prepared to use this strategy includes:

1.   After the stock has gone through a bullish trend, you will see that the prices will reach a peak, and then there will be a decline. The decline that occurs is going to form a trough.

2.   Then the price will rise again a little bit in order to form a second high, one that is actually quite a bit above the first peak, but then it will decline down again.

3.   The price will come back up a third time. but it won't go higher; it will simply go to the same height, or similar, as the first peak before it declines down once more.

The first and the third peak are going to be the shoulders, and the second peak is going to form the head. And then there is a line that will connect together the first and second troughs, and this is known as the neckline.

You will find that it is possible to work with this kind of trend in order to see whether there is a downward trend that is about to happen, and that can help you to know when the prices are about to go back down. If you are worried about the prices going down because you own some of the stocks, this is a great way to get out of the market and maintain your profits. But if you are trying to get into the market, you would want to look for one of these to tell whether it was a good time to enter the market or not.

Working With the Moving Average

The next option that we will take a look at is the moving average trend. This is a good one that helps us to know whether a security is about to go up or down, and can help us to see the best time to enter into a trade and the best time to get out. This is important because it is a good way to be prepared and come up with the plan that you want to use on a variety of different securities.

Remember that there are many stocks out there that you can choose from, and many of them will have their own morning trend that you can watch for, either going up or down really strong. You would then want to watch their charts and see where the moving averages head on the charts. This can be a beneficial thing to work with because the trader simply needs to watch these moving averages to learn more about how the trend is occurring. Then they can jump in at the right times and ride it out until they make profits.

While it is a strategy that takes a bit of time to learn and will require you to really watch the data that comes with it, you will find that this is one of the best options that you can choose to go with as well. There are a number of steps that we are able to follow in order to make this one work well, and some of them include:

- When you take a look at the graphs that you want to use, and you are checking out the stock you want to use, make sure that you look to see whether or not a trend is forming near the spot that is the moving average. When you do see this, you will want to get into the market and use this strategy. You can then spend a bit of time looking at the trading data that shows up for that stock from the day before. This is important to see how the moving average changes and how the stock is going to respond to that average.

- After looking over the charts, and getting a chance to see which moving average is the best one for the trade you are doing, it is time to make a purchase of the stock. Some traders do choose to wait a little bit longer in order to confirm the moving average before they enter. But either way, try to purchase as close to the lines for the moving average as you can.

- Once you are ready, you need to pick out the stop points that you want to use. You may want to consider setting the stop just a bit below the moving average line to help protect your investment, but it still allows for a little bit of volatility of movement. If you are doing this strategy with a candlestick chart, then you need to make sure that you have a start that is close to the moving average, and choose to work with a long position.

- After you have these in place and have been able to enter the market, you can just ride on that trend until you see the moving average break, and then take your profits.

When we handle this kind of strategy, we have to remember that we should not work with something known as a trailing stop. This is also a strategy where we need to pay and give our full attention to the market, and it is usually more than what the other strategies will ask for because it is possible that the market can move quickly, and it will get away from you. While the scanner is going to work well for helping you to get the right trades, we have to make sure that we are working with our own eyes, rather than relying on the scanner, especially when we work with this kind of strategy.

If you are looking at some of the charts and what they are telling us, and you see that the security you chose is going really far up from the moving average, this means that you are earning a good deal of profit. At this time, it may be in your best interest to take the half position rather than going to the full break. This will help you to walk away with some profits rather than nothing and can help you to avoid losing money if the trend decides to reverse itself. With the half position, if you reach it, you will still walk away with something

The Resistance Trading Method

Now it is time for us to dive right into our next strategy and how this will help us to take the stock market and earn a good profit on it. This is going to be one that will work with support and resistance and how we can harness those to make a lot of money. There are a bunch of other swing traders who work with this, so you will have some good company if you choose to go with it as well. The support is going to be what the price level is when the buyer is really strong, so strong that it is able to reverse or even interrupt a current downtrend that is on the graphs at that time.

When you are looking at a downtrend on the charts, and you notice that it gets to a specific support level, which is basically a place on the charts where the sock doesn't seem to get lower than at all, it will do a little bounce. The bounce is sometimes really big and sometimes really small, so it really depends on how the market is doing. When you look at your charts, you should see that this support line is going to be on the bottom, going horizontally, and it has to touch at least two of your bottoms before it can count.

In addition to spending some time on the support, we have to take a look at the resistance as well. this is going to basically be the opposite of what we talked about with the support bar. This is going to be the high price level that shows us that the position of selling is strong, one that is able to gain enough strength that it reverses the uptrend, at least a little bit.

Any time that you notice an uptrend get to this level, you should know that the trend is going to stop there, in most cases, and sometimes it will start to go down. Just like with the support, sometimes it will go down a lot and sometimes just a little bit. The resistance is something that is shown just like with the support, but it is able to connect two or more tops to it.

There are also some trading situations where it is possible to get support or resistance that is minor. These will cause a trend to pause a bit. But if you work with some of the major resistances and supports as we mentioned before, then this is strong enough to take our trend and force it into reverse. Traders who work with this strategy need to try and figure out how to purchase as close to the support as they can, and then they need to sell that position as close to the line of resistance as possible. This will be the best way to get the most profits out of that trade.

To make this strategy work, we need to figure out the levels of support and resistance. And to do this, we need to bring out a few daily charts that have our chosen stocks on this. Sometimes the line is a bit hard to find, and you need to look through a few days to see what is the best option and get a line that is clear enough you feel comfortable with using it. This means to get the most out of this trading strategy; you need to have some patience and keep your emotions in check.

Along with this, there are a few steps that we are able to use as long as we are able to pull out a few charts and graphs to help us get through this. Some of the steps that you can use to make this process easier and to make sure we get the most out of this strategy include:

- Remember talking about indecision candles at some point in your studies f swing trading? You are going to see these in areas of support and resistance. These candles often show that buys and sellers are fighting with each other to see who has the most control over the price.

- Often half dollars and whole dollars can be good support and resistance levels. This is especially true when you work on stocks under $10. If you can't find your support or your resistance lines, check here and see if your line would work there.

- When you make your own lines, you need to have the most recent data available. This ensures that you are getting the best information for that stock.

- The more that your line is able to touch the extreme price of the stock, the better option this line is for your support and resistance. If it is too far from this extreme point, then it is not going to have enough value to make it strong.

- Only look at any support or resistance lines that stay with the current price range. For example, if the stock's price is around $20 right now, you do not need to look at the region on the graph where the stock randomly jumped up to $40. This is not an area where the stock will probably go back to, so it doesn't make much sense to work from there.

- Many times the support and resistance are not just one exact number. Often it is more of an area. If you come up with a support or resistance that is about $19.69, then you know that the movement is somewhere near that number, not exactly that number. You can usually estimate that the area is going to be somewhere between five to ten cents above or under that line.

- The price that you want to work from will need to have a clear bounce off that level. If you can't find that this price bounces at that level, then this is not a good support or resistance level for you to work with. Your levels need to be really easy to notice and need to make sense of the charts you look at. If you have any questions about whether you picked the right one or not, it's not the right one.

When you head over to some of your charts and create the lines that you need for this strategy, it is easy to see that drawing the perfect line the whole time is a bit of a challenge. You have to use some caution when you pick the lines because there are so many variables, and you are basing all of your decisions on this as well. you need to go with the ones that make the most sense for your data, or you could really throw the work out.

The best way to do this is to get some practice. Look at a lot of different charts and graphs and get familiar with how they work and where the support and resistance would be. It is only as difficult as you make it, and the more practice you get with these, the easier it is to write in some of these lines that you can actually follow.

Opening Range Breakout

Another strategy that we can spend our time on is the opening range breakout. This is a good strategy because it does provide us with some good signals on when to enter the market, but sometimes there is an added challenge of knowing when you should get out of the process and take your profit. You do need to put in some elbow grease with this one and figure out the best place for this based on your own research, and you can even pick out how much profit you would like to make on the trade as long as it is realistic.

To work with this strategy, you have to really pay some good attention to what is happening in the market, and you have to be prepared to jump in right away. When you take a look at a few of the stock charts, you may see that a few of the socks in play (okay, most of them) are going to have some really violent price action in one direction or another.

The reason for this is that the buyers and the sellers are trying to flood into the market during the first few minutes when it is open. This is a crazy time for us to trade. New investors will often stay out of the market right here because there is a lot of volatility that shows up, and sometimes that is a lot for a beginner to handle.

However, as you get more experience with the market and learn more about how it works, it is possible to join in on this market rush and make some good money. If you are someone who panics with this, you need to be careful. It is a volatile time, and there are situations where you will be wrong and lose out on money in a short amount of time.

This is a time period where a lot of investors are going to panic and then sell their stocks because they think they need to regain their positions right away. Then there are some beginners who are not used to the market, and they will jump on as well for the discount or jump out because they are scared as well. both of these are important movements to watch because they will help us to get a better look at the price of the stock, and can tell us more about what will happen in the proceeding day as well.

Remember though all of this that you are working as a swing trader, it is usually best for you to stay out of the market and not jump into the opening range breakout. This is a method that can work, but it is so volatile, and it doesn't always go in the direction that you would like. Waiting about fifteen minutes, or a least a bit to see where the trend is settling down, is a much better option.

The reason that we want to wait a bit here is that it is so easy to get stuck in some of the craziness of the morning changes in the market, and you do not want to get the wrong ideas and get stuck on the wrong end of things either. You can wait just a few minutes, watching a few of the stocks that you favor, and still jump in without missing out on some of the great opportunities that will show up.

Like a lot of the other strategies that we have taken the time to talk about through our guidebook, the opening range strategy is going to work the best if you have some large stocks or mid-cap stocks that will not end up with some unpredictable price swings when you decide to hold onto them. You also want to be careful and not go with this strategy if you see some stocks that are low float. The best option is to choose stocks that can trade inside a range that is smaller than what we see with the Average True Range, or the ATR.

With some of that in mind, we need to walk through some of the steps that we can follow in order to get the most out of swing trading with this strategy. Some of the steps that we can use include:

- After you have had some time to create your watchlist in the morning, you should wait until the stock market has time to settle down, so wait for about five minutes. During this time, watch the price action and the opening range.

257

You can also check out how many shares are traded during that time and then figure out from that information if the stock is going down or up. This time is when a ton of orders go through the market, and you want to look at these numbers to see how liquid a stock actually is.

- During this time, you can also look through to see what the ATR of that stock is. you want the opening range to be smaller compared to the ATR, so make sure the ATR number is nearby.

- Once those first five minutes of market opening are finished, you may see that the stock will stay in that opening range a bit longer depending on what traders and investors want to do. However, if you see at this time that the stock is breaking out of this range, it time to enter the trade. Enter the trade going the same direction of the breakout. If you can, go long if you see the breakout is going up, but go short if the breakout is going down.

- Pick out a good target for your profit as well. You can find this by looking at the daily levels from the previous day and identify where the stock is before the market opens. You can also look at the previous days' close, along with the moving averages, to come up with a good target.

- If you can't find the right technical level for your chosen target or for the exit, you can choose to go long and then look for signs of weakness. On the other hand, if you want to take a short position, and then the stock goes high, this shows you the stock is strong, and you want to cover the position as much as you can.

This is a good strategy for a swing trader to work on if they want to have a short time frame, but it also works well with some of those longer time frames as well. Keep in mind here, that the steps we just went through above are done with some shorter trades that are only a day or two long. But it is simple enough to go through and expand it out a bit more to ensure you get the right amount of time for your trades.

The Interesting Red to Green Strategy

Now it is time for us to move on and take a look at a strategy that we can use known as the red to green strategy. The name of this one may sound a little funny, but it is a great option to make sure that you are prepared and can really catch some of the movements that will show up in your stocks. This strategy will require that you can look through some of the historical data that shows up for your stocks and then use that to figure out how you should react and which ways you should invest.

This one is going to have a really good look at some of the historical information because that is what will tell us what the stock has done in the past, and can give us a better idea of what it is likely to do in the future. While you are searching through some graphs and some of this historical data, it is important that you pay at least a little attention to some of the current prices of the stocks that you are interested in. If you do this and then notice that the price is higher than it was the day before, then this is a good indicator that the price is going up, and that will turn a green day over to a red day. What this will mean for us is that the percentage of the price change will end up being negative, and that shows up as red in our charts.

We can also take this the other way if we would like, which would mean that we go from a red to green day in some cases. It all depends on what information we are finding in our charts along the way.

The strategy that we have to work with here to make sure that our method works the way that we want, whether we go from green to red or red to green. To make this easier to understand, we will just stick with one of the options and look at the steps, and then you can make some adjustments to make sure that it works going the other way as well.

For this one, we will spend some time looking at how to go from a red to a green day, which is a common way to use this. To make sure that you use this strategy well, the steps that we have to follow will include:

- When you get up in the morning and are ready to start trading, and you are working on your watchlist, you need to make sure that you are pulling up information that comes from the previous day as well. Make sure that you specifically look at the closing information, checking out what the price action was at that time.

- If you see these chars and see that the stock is moving to where it was before on the previous close, this means that you will want to go along with that strategy. You can use your profit target from the previous day to set yourself up well.

- When setting up your stop loss on this strategy, you should be as close to the technical level as you can. This means that if you made a purchase at a support line, then make sure that the stop loss ends up being near where that support line was as well.

- It is also a good idea to come up with a profit target and then stick with it during the trade. It is going to help you to see the best results and will ensure that you can walk away with at least some sort of profit in the end.

This is a great strategy to work with if you have some of the historical data about your business, and you are excited to use it to your advantage. And you can definitely use it when the market is going in the other direction as well, which is going to make it one of the best strategies to learn because there is so much that we are able to do with it!

The Gap up, Inside Bar, and Then Breakout

The final one that we are going to work on here is a bit more complex than some of the others, but that is part of the fun of working with it as well. We are going to spend some time learning how to read the graphs with this one to ensure we see exactly what we think we do, and that way we can make some more in profits along the way. This is a trading signal that we work with, and you need to pull out the charts and see if there is some gap up in the process. Then, if you see that there is a second or a third ten-minute bar that also shows up here and it turns into what looks like an inside bar, you are set to go. This is going to be the setup that you need in order to make this particular strategy behave the way that you want.

Now, there are some traders who like to work with this particular strategy, but they make some changes to it. They will work with a few stocks that have a partial gap in place rather than one that has the full gap that we talked about. When we are on the search for that partial gap instead, you will need to look for a setup where the gap is higher than it was on the close for that stock on the previous day, or it is not going to work the way that we want.

In addition, we have to also make sure that the partial gap we are looking for will come in lower than the high of the previous day as well. the reason for this is that it will provide you with some good signals to show that this stock is a good one, but it also makes certain that along the way, you have a few good options to work with compared to waiting around for the full gap. You a choice whether you would like to work on the full gap or the partial gap, but the partial gap is sometimes seen as a safer alternative to work with.

When you are working with this strategy, you want to keep the charts to a minimum time frame. For example, you may only want to go with one or two of these ten-minute bars before you start with your inside bar. Beware though. If you see that there are more than these two ten-minute bars, it means that the price has had way too much movement at this point, and you should avoid this option because it isn't the most effective setup.

As soon as you have the right inside the bar, without too much volatility going on in the market, it is time to purchase your stop. Make sure that this stop is right about the high you see in your bar. The trigger is the breakout that is above your inside bar.

When you get to this point, it is possible that you need to be patient and wait a bit. We want to search around and find the right trade signal that can allow us to go long. Then, if you have your stop in place at the right time, you will need to think more about some of the logistics of your plan and how this will all work out. Keep it all in order and keep the stop loss points in the right place, and this strategy will work out great for you.

As we can see, there is a lot that we are able to love about working in swing trading, and there are a lot of great strategies that we can pick and choose from based on what meets our needs the best. When we can put all of this together, we can certainly use it to make some good profits in the stock market, or in any other market that we want, even as a beginner.

CHAPTER 7

TIPS TO GET THE MOST OUT OF THE SWING TRADING

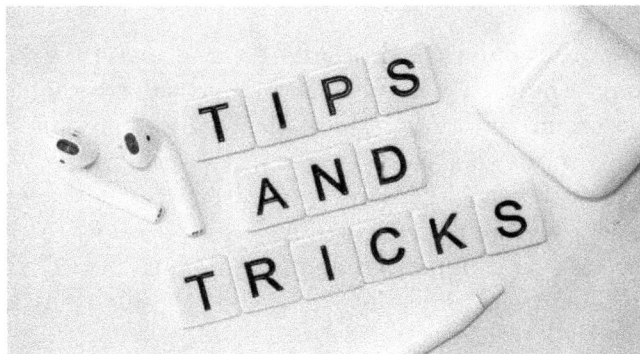

Now that we have had some time to look at how to work in swing trading and all the great benefits that come with this, it is time for us to move on and look at a few of the different tips and tricks that we can use in order to see some great results. These tips will make sure that you can trade like a professional in no time, even if you haven't had a chance to work with swing trading or other types of stock market trading in the past. Some of the tips that we can follow to see the best results with our swing trading endeavors includes:

Pick Out a Stop Loss Point

One of the first things that you need to consider when working on some of your trades is where you would like to place your stop-loss points. There should be one that will pull you out of the market if the prices get too low and you start losing money, and then another one for the number of profits that you want to make, which will pull you out of the market when that number has been reached as well.

This needs to be as important to your plan as the entry point. These are your protections and will ensure that you are in and out of the market before you end up losing money and increasing your risk too much. The stock market, especially when it comes to swing trading, can be risky, so you have to learn how to cut that risk to a minimum as much as possible. These stop-loss points are going to be the best way to make this risk lower.

First, we want to set up our stop loss point for losing money. There are times when the market is not going to behave the way that we would like, and it turns downward, so we start to lose money. Our emotions can get into the mix and then we see our money slipping through our fingers. We get worried about this and we want to make the money back. So we stay in the market too long or we make some bad decisions, even if the charts and graphs are showing us exactly what we should do. We refuse to give up, and we may lose more money than necessary for this.

The stop loss point will help to prevent this kind of issue. You can set it right when you get in the market, thinking logically about how much money you would be comfortable losing on this trade if things don't go well. You will set this, and then if the market does reach that, it will kick your orders out, and you will get to regroup and restart later on. It is as simple as that and can help to reduce the amount of risk that you are dealing with along the way.

We also need to make sure that we place a stop loss in place for how much profit we can make as well. this may seem silly because we would all answer that we want to make as much money as possible, so why would we want to put one of these in place to limit our risk.

Unfortunately, it is not likely that the potential profit is going to be unlimited when we go with swing trading on the stock market, so that is not something that we should concentrate on at all. We need to always look at all trades and consider how much profits we would be happy with if the trade is successful. And then we need to put the stop loss there.

The way that this helps us is that it ensures we make some kind of profit if we enter the market and that we don't lose our profits in the process. It is too easy for us to get to the target profit, and then the market goes down, and we lose out on it all. This is another thing that the emotions can influence, and if we lose out on all of the profits, we will sure miss that profit instead. Add this in ahead of time to make sure that you can walk away from the trade with some profits.

Set Aside Money to Invest

It is important that you never invest money that you can't afford to use. It is easy to hear that there is a great option out there, one that you have to jump in right now, and you are guaranteed to make a lot of money on in the process. And so, because you trust that person so well and you know there is no way that you will lose, you put all of your savings and money towards the house on it and hope for the big money and the new lifestyle to come out.

But then things don't work out, and you end up losing a lot of money in the process. That big lead was all false, and the market takes a big turn. This is even more likely because you didn't take the time to learn about the market and what it can offer in the process. You lose everything, and now you are struggling to find money to pay the mortgage or any of the other things that you are hoping to get paid that month.

This is kind of extreme to think about, but it still shows us the importance of only investing what we can afford at the time. When you invest too much, or more than you can afford, then you will bring the emotions into the game, and that can be a dangerous thing to work with overall. It is much better to leave those emotions at the door or you make bad decisions that will lead you to failure.

Instead of investing money that you can' really afford, a better option to use is to set aside a separate savings account. The only money that goes into this account is the money that is for investing. It is not money that is earmarked to work for your mortgage, your insurance, your food, or anything else. It is extra money that is left in your budget and can be used for some of your investment without any worry about it being gone.

While none of us wants to lose money, of course, this is much safer to work with. Even if it is a small amount, it is money that is safe to play with and doesn't have any additional ties to it that you need to worry about. This means that you are able to use it, and if you are working on a strategy and it doesn't behave the way that you want, then the money won't be as big of a deal. Once the money is gone for that month out of the account, then you are done investing until the next month, or at least until you can put more money into the account. Don't let your investments cause you to live without, or you will end up with a lot of emotions in the process.

Keep the Emotions Out

The best thing that you can do when working on swing trading is to learn how to keep the emotions out of the game. Your emotions are going to be your worst enemy in all of this, and if you choose to add them in or you aren't able to block them out, then you will lose more money than you can ever make in the process. This is a hard one for a lot of people, and this is why many of them decide to not stick with trading at all.

The first thing to realize with this one is that you will lose money sometimes. Sometimes you will not understand what the market is doing, and you will make the wrong decisions. Sometimes you will not understand how to work with the strategy that you picked, and that can make you lose money. And sometimes the market just does something that no one was expecting and that makes a lot of investors, even those who are more experienced, lose money in the process as well.

If you have that realization in your mind from the start, then this can help you to stay calm and see some good results in the process. In fact, this is one of the best ways to make sure that when a loss happens, you will not be overwhelmed or feel like you need to stay in the market for too long. The stop-loss points that we talked about earlier will come in and make a big difference. They can get put in right at the beginning before you have a chance to let the emotions show up and cause some problems. Then the system will execute the plan or the strategy that you put in place, and it will help you to be situated and ready to go without all the emotions clouding your judgment.

Learn a Few Good Strategies and Stick With Them

We spent a lot of time in the previous chapter looking at some of the best strategies that you can use with swing trading, and really with lots of the trading methods that you want to use if you decide to branch out later. All of them work in slightly different manners, and it often depends on how the market is going, what the stocks are doing, and how much volatility is found in the market as a whole.

All of the strategies that we talked about in this guidebook are going to be legitimate ones that traders will use on a regular basis. This means that if you find the right market conditions, you can use any of them and earn some good profits in the process. There are times when they will fail, but this is more about the market moving in ways that you were not expecting, and not that there is something wrong with this strategy in the first place.

This means that you have a lot of really great options that you are able to work with, ones that will make it so much easier for you to figure out how the market is working and how you can make money. There are even options that will work well whether you want to look for an upward trend or the downward trend in the market at the time. You have to choose which works for you.

As a trader, the market is going to change on you quite a bit, so you need to have at least a handful of options available that you are comfortable with. This will greatly expand your reach in the market and can help you to be prepared for all kinds of market conditions based on what works the best at that time. The more of these you know how to do, the better as well. But working with just a few of them at a time, and then expanding out to more as you gain more familiarity, can really make a big difference as well.

You can choose any of thee strategies that you would like to work with. There are many in the previous chapter that can help you to get into the market at the right time to see some results. You can also look and do some of your research in order to find some of the ones that you would like. But pick out two or three options that you are comfortable with using and work from there to get the best results in the process with your trading and to help you prepare for all kinds of situations.

Don't Switch Strategies While In a Trade

One thing that we need to remember is that when we enter into a trade, we need to stick with it. This can be hard. Many beginners will get started with a trade, and insist on switching to a new strategy that they didn't start with in the first place. This is one of the worst things that you can do for your success in the stock market, so you have to avoid it.

If you go through and find that one of the strategies you are using is not providing you with any success, then this is a sign that it is time to get out of the trade and get out of it. This is hard sometimes. We want to work with a strategy that is going to win. But sometimes, even the best traders end up losing money, and you need to know when it is time to get out and try something else. Sometimes a strategy will not work the way that we want, and we just need to get out and try a new trade later on.

It is really easy for a beginner to get into the trade and then not follow this rule. They see a trade that looks good and like it would work well with the strategy that they picked. But after they get in the market, things reverse and don't work the way that they want. Then they will go through and try to switch their strategy and try out a few other things. Whether they just wing it along the way or they pick out another strategy instead, they make changes right in the middle of the trade. This will barely go well for you.

Changing your strategy is never a good thing to work with at all. This is just asking for things to go wrong. You are not planning things out and thinking it through when you do this, and that can lead to some dangerous trades that will keep you from making the money that you want in the process. Even if the trade does not go the way that you want, it is best to start with one trade and stick with it until the trade is done. When that trade is done, you can always go back and try a different strategy later on.

There are a lot of options that you are able to work with for swing trading. This is very important to understand, and you have to learn which one works the best for the market conditions that you see. But never go through and switch from one strategy to the next when you are already doing a trade.

These tips are going to be so important to ensure that we are going to get the best results overall here. It is hard to get into the stock market, especially when we work with a shorter-term option like swing trading. You need to make some smart decisions, you need to make sure that your emotions are not getting in the way, and you need to think through all of the decisions that you do at the time. When you are ready to get into the market, and you want to see how great it can be for your needs, make sure to follow these tips to help improve your rate of success.

CONCLUSION

Congratulation on making it through to the end of Swing Trading, let's hope it was informative and able to provide you with all of the tools you need to achieve your goals whatever they may be.

The next step is to jump right in and get ready to do some of the tradings on your own. We took a lot of time to look more at this kind of investment strategy and what we are able to do with it as well. this is a simple strategy, and it can really bring in a ton of results. But sometimes looking through all of this information can be a challenge, and figuring out where to start is not always as simple as it seems.

The goal here is to help show you how easy swing trading can be and why it is one of the best options to make sure that you are set and ready to go when it is time to put your money to work for you. We went through the steps that are necessary to get the trade going, as well as a lot of the different strategies that you can use along the way to make sure you get in and out of the market at the right times.

There are going to be sometimes when you lose money. That is just the way that this process works, and even those who have been in the market for a long time will be able to lose on occasion. As you get more practice with swing trading and the strategies that you like to use, you will find that this process gets better, and you will get more wins overall.

Swing trading is one of the best options that you can use when it is time to invest your money and put it to work for you. When you are ready to learn more about swing trading and what it can do for you, make sure to check out this guidebook to get started.

Finally, if you found this book useful in anyway, a review on Amazon is always appreciated!

www.ingramcontent.com/pod-product-compliance
Lightning Source LLC
Chambersburg PA
CBHW061023220326
41597CB00019BB/3153